INVITATION TO ARCHITECTURE

INVITATION TO
ARCHITECTURE

DISCOVERING DELIGHT *in the* WORLD BUILT AROUND US

MAX JACOBSON
with SHELLEY BROCK

The Taunton Press

The Taunton Press
Inspiration for hands-on living®

The Taunton Press, Inc.
63 South Main Street, PO Box 5506
Newtown, CT 06470-5506
e-mail: tp@taunton.com

Editor: Peter Chapman
Copy editor: Seth Reichgott
Indexer: Jay Kreider
Cover and interior design: carol singer | notice design
Layout: carol singer | notice design
Illustrators: Max Jacobson and Shelley Brock

The following names/manufacturers appearing in *Invitation to Architecture* are trademarks:
7-Eleven®, Barbie®, Frisbee®, Jello®, Mattel®, Sim-City®, YouTube™

Library of Congress Cataloging-in-Publication Data

Jacobson, Max, 1941-
  Invitation to architecture : discovering delight in the world built around us /
Max Jacobson.
     pages cm
   ISBN 978-1-62113-837-2 (hardback)
 1. Architecture. I. Title.
  NA2550.J33 2014
  720--dc23
                         2014005503

PRINTED IN THE UNITED STATES OF AMERICA

10 9 8 7 6 5 4 3 2 1

ACKNOWLEDGMENTS

OUR MOST INFLUENTIAL TEACHERS during our architectural educations included Christopher Alexander, Richard Peters, and Daniel Solomon at UC Berkeley, and Kenneth Frampton, Peter Testa, and Richard Plunz at Columbia University.

Since then there have been many architects whose work we have found inspiring: Renzo Piano, Carlo Scarpa, Steven Holl, Bernard Maybeck, Julia Morgan, and Lou Kahn, to name just a few; while some of our most challenging influences (and spurs to our thinking) have been Palladio and Peter Eisenman.

We have been privileged to work with and learn from William McDonough in New York, Beverley Spears in Santa Fe, and, for 35 years, the JSWD architectural firm with Murray Silverstein, Barbara Winslow, and Helen Degenhardt in Berkeley.

The writers that most directly inspired, informed, and engaged us as we worked on this book (besides Vitruvius) include Jane Jacobs, Mario Salvadori, Gaston Bachelard, John Ruskin, Stanley Abercrombie, Vincent Scully, Stewart Brand, Lisa Heschong, Paul Goldberger, Michael Pollan, Forrest Wilson, and Robert Mark.

We are especially grateful to the several friendly critics who agreed to read our developing manuscript for their insightful comments and encouragement: Chuck Miller (our first reader, who urged us to send the early manuscript to The Taunton Press), Murray Silverstein, Lorraine Lupo, Juri Komendant, Jen Taylor, and Rene Watkins. And a special thanks to Helen Degenhardt who gave us the critical, temporal, and physical space (in the house and office) to work on this project.

We did the drawings in a variety of styles to illustrate the range of sketches that are useful in design thinking and also included a couple of guest drawings: Karen Fiene's memories of childhood building with blankets and chairs, and Forrest Wilson's wonderful personified sketch of Gothic cathedral structure.

Thanks to David Miller, who so generously toured us through his firm's Bullitt Center in Seattle. And thanks to the staff of The Taunton Press—especially our editor Peter Chapman, who encouraged us to develop our rough draft into a book.

Finally, we want to dedicate this book to our students who, over many years, often asked questions that we felt we could answer, but most important, asked questions we couldn't, inviting us to become students alongside them.

TABLE OF CONTENTS

INTRODUCTION

THIS BOOK IS AN INVITATION TO ARCHITECTURE: an invitation to recall your first encounters with it, to explore its presence in your immediate environment, to examine the elements that transform mere building into architecture, and to discover how it shapes our lives in ways we may not be aware of. We write for all who want to know more about what architecture offers to our lives.

This book is also offered as a guide to those who are already interested in the design of buildings and who wonder whether architecture might be a career choice worth considering. They may want an opportunity to learn whether architecture is a possible profession for them before committing to a college major. This volume should help them decide. The same is true not only of undergraduates but also of adults who are considering a return to college to finish a degree in architecture or who have decided to change careers. This book will be helpful to a homeowner, as well as to a member of a design committee who as a layperson is working on a project with an architect and welcomes a deeper understanding of how the designer thinks and works.

We emphasize the appreciation and understanding of architecture for a very wide cross section of the population because we know that although only a few will go on to become practicing architects, everyone lives in the built environment and is deeply affected by it. The more people become interested in and knowledgeable about architecture, the more vital and effective role they can play in what gets preserved, what gets torn down, rebuilt, or reused, and what is newly created.

The creation of architecture is arguably based on the widest range of knowledge, skill, and experience of any human activity. It involves looking at and understanding how we use our spaces and places and what they mean to us. It also involves understanding the nature of building materials and the many environmental impacts of building. The making of architecture also requires us to respect and to work within certain limitations: those of physics and chemistry, those imposed by our society and its laws, and those presented by a homeowner or a building owner's wishes, needs, and financial capacities. And beyond all of this, architecture also plays a role in producing aesthetic, emotional, and perhaps even intellectual pleasure in our environment. A tall order indeed. Modern architectural schools try to address the need for such a broad preparation by requiring courses in math and science, architecture history, structures, graphics, mechanical systems, and professional practice, all in addition to an intensive design studio process. But what should come first? Where is the best place to begin this exciting and complex undertaking? What should be offered in an introductory course in architecture?

As teachers of introductory courses in architecture, we find ourselves in the position of inviting new students into a focus of study that can be a first step toward a profession that we have been practicing for many years. These students range from those few already committed to pursuing the field through all the many steps required for licensing, to the majority who are simply exploring the possibility that they may find architecture interesting, something they may want to know more about. As we begin each new semester, we ask the questions mentioned above, as well as, "What fundamental skills do they need now that can be developed as they pursue further studies in design?" One way we try to answer these questions is by examining our own student experience: "What did I learn as a beginning student of architecture that, in retrospect, has proven essential?" "What was presented that has not been so helpful?" and finally, "What was missing that I should have been introduced to in my early architectural classes?"

At the core of this inquiry is this underlying question: What is architecture really all about? Are all buildings examples of architecture? We all agree that the Parthenon exemplifies architecture, but what about my house, my school, my workplace, or my supermarket? Do they also qualify as examples? An invitation to architecture needs to start by addressing this question. Failing to answer it can lead to wildly divergent and eccentric views of what architecture consists of, ranging from an idea that only famous architects produce architecture, to the belief that only huge and expensive buildings are examples, or that only controversial and very unique buildings qualify. On the other hand, some conclude that only traditional indigenous cultures are capable of creating genuine architecture, and that modern structures by architects are artificial and hollow echoes of the real architecture of the past.

To complicate things further, the last 200 years of architectural education and theory have generated dramatically different and rapidly changing concepts of what constitutes good architecture. Even during the last 30 years the field has gone through a half-dozen "theories" of architecture. We will discuss these in some detail in a later chapter, but here we simply want to point out the difficulty these trends create for a public trying to understand and appreciate architecture.

This turbulent sea of architectural theory and practice creates a quandary for our society at large, and for both students of architecture and their teachers and guides. Many contemporary buildings are so novel and unrelated to more familiar structures that one doesn't know how to relate to them or to evaluate one's feelings toward them. As a lay person this can make you feel foolish wondering why you're not "getting" the building. Architectural journals and books often don't help to further our understanding because they tend to engage in an arcane, "professional insider" discourse that is sometimes bandied about to defend or attack these various contemporary approaches. Even the reviews of new buildings by architectural critics that appear in the media often speak more to the intelligentsia and the specialized culture of architects and their clients than they do to the wider public who will live with the new buildings and who often wish they could better understand these structures.

Those of us who practice architecture and are trying to do a good job of teaching and explaining our work to our clients and the general public face our own difficulties. Architectural theory and practice is so volatile that much of what we learned in design school, and what we took from it into our practice, is no longer at the forefront of change. If we matriculated in the late 1960s, architectural theory may have focused on social and psychological issues in architecture, such as the potential influence of our designs on crime, or on the users' sense of safety. In terms of practice, we designed our buildings using pencil and hand-drafting. European training in the 1970s emphasized structure and materials (using ink on vellum). But if we went to school in the 1980s and 1990s, architectural theory emphasized specific messages of form (and we designed using the pencil, multi-media collage, and models, but often presented using 3-D software).

Some aspects of these approaches continue to be taught in the schools of architecture, but for the most part the students attending today's architecture schools have been swept up in a digital revolution along with the rest of the world. Many recent architecture design programs offered at colleges and universities tend to focus on the creation of computer-generated form, sometimes overlooking pertinent social and psychological issues or even the function and meaning of the resulting forms. The outcome of this environment of rapidly changing ideas and design approaches is that we teachers of architecture—with

5

our various training and practice histories—don't generally agree on which theory should be taught and will each emphasize our own brand of approach. Unfortunately, this situation can cause real confusion among students and the general public interested in contemporary architecture. Still, this plurality of points of view, although often confusing, can end up being beneficial to students of architecture in the long run by allowing them to compare the different approaches and to eventually come up with their own responses. But this situation still leaves the general public at a loss as to how to make sense of the newest buildings that appear in our environment.

We teachers of architecture have an additional problem: Although some of us are producing cutting-edge projects that might receive international attention, the practical experience of most is limited to more modest works, to projects where we are members of a client-contractor team, not the "starchitect." It is from this relatively modest scope of expertise that we can most confidently and effectively teach and talk about architecture. Teachers of architecture who are also engaged in professional practice (just like academic lawyers and doctors who are also practicing) tend to teach what is essential to their current work, not to forecast what will be important in the future. This is probably not as great a disadvantage as it sounds, given the fact that our students will most likely begin practice in an office working as part of a team under the direction of others, not as independent architects. Although we can best teach what we have been able to successfully practice, our students will gradually find themselves in a new and different set of conditions in the work world, with different issues and different required skills.

Finally, we must admit that we practitioners and teachers are ourselves not always so sure about what precisely is so important about architecture, what it means, and how to look at it. What we may have fervently believed as young, idealistic architects is inevitably tempered and modified as we mature. Hopefully our ideas and goals are broadening, becoming more whole and encompassing a wider range of relevant issues. We too are learning and growing, searching, along with our clients and students, for deeper and more inclusive understandings of the role of architecture in our lives.[1]

And so we come back to our original questions: "What are the most important concepts that need to be presented during an introductory course in architecture?" And "When I was a beginning student of architecture, what was missing that I should have been introduced to in my early architectural classes?" This book is our tentative answer.

In Chapter 1, we'll consider the many ways architecture influences our lives, from our activities as young children to our everyday interests and interactions as adults, whether we tend to identify them as "architecture" or not. By becoming more aware of our own actions and experiences, we'll address the need to help students (and ourselves) tune in to and become more receptive to the various influences that the environment and its buildings have on us. This encourages us to take the time not only to notice the architecture that may already be around us but also to hear, feel, and listen to its messages.

This level of focused attention is an important aspect of any true act of appreciation. But what is it, exactly, that we are looking for? The best approach is to try not to look for anything in particular at first, but simply to begin to notice how different spaces feel to us. How does a certain place change throughout the day or season, or when do we feel a safe sense of enclosure and when do we feel uncomfortable or disoriented in relation to our surroundings? Once we are more attentive to our environment we naturally begin to distinguish between positive and negative influences, between what works well and what seems to frustrate, what endures and what deteriorates. We all stand to gain a new and beneficial way of seeing if we can awaken to the ways we interact with the world around us.

---

[1]As an example, the exhibit "Palladio in America" traveled around the country in the late 1960s, and in those politically left-leaning schools of architecture that emphasized social and psychological issues the wooden models of the villas seemed cold, impersonal, and uncomfortably formal. Subsequent tours of the actual buildings, with their structural integrity, clear functionality, and geometric and proportional harmony, proved how rewarding and architecturally important these buildings were and remain.

Once we are paying closer attention, we can explore what differentiates "architecture" from mere "building," as we do in Chapter 2. As a profession, architecture has goals and ethics. Like medicine, it strives to improve both physical and mental health, safety, and pleasure in life. Architecture serves clients, the people who want to build buildings as well as the people who use them. In doing so, it must not only address direct requests and immediate needs but also uncover unspoken yearnings in order to address those underlying longer-term needs that may not at first be apparent to the client. The profession takes responsibility for its works, guaranteeing certain levels of adequacy and performance. This sense of service to society builds on the deeper intention that makes architecture the vital human endeavor that it is. Architecture aspires to a higher level of satisfaction than mere building, and it is important for students to understand this from the outset. Once architecture's goals and aspirations are illuminated, all the ages of architecture, periods, styles, and fads can be more clearly evaluated and understood in this light.

During the Roman Empire at the end of the 1st century B.C.E. the architect Vitruvius[2] worked as a loyal subject of Emperor Augustus, designing fortifications and bridges as well as buildings. In his *Ten Books on Architecture,* completed between c. 30 and 20 B.C.E., Vitruvius wrote that architecture must achieve three interrelated goals: to be firm in its physical structure, to be useful in its design, and to be beautiful.[3]

This triumvirate of *firmitas, utilitas,* and *venustas,* to use the original Latin terms coined by Vitruvius (later translated into English as firmness, commodity, and delight by Sir Henry Wotton in 1624), remains the core concept of what architecture strives for, and when

---

[2] His full name was Marcus Vitruvius Pollio.

[3] Vitruvius's words were, "[Buildings] must be built with due reference to durability, convenience, and beauty." These words are from the Morgan translation of 1914. His *Ten Books on Architecture* have been fundamental to the architecture of the Western World.

successful raises the level of its creations above less ambitious "background buildings."[4]

This ancient formula is as relevant today as it was in Rome. Using this three-legged conceptual platform as a guide for our thinking, we will flesh it out to account for how we understand the terms today, reinterpreting and embellishing the triad to address the realities of contemporary life and culture. This firm base, then, allows us to lay a foundation for a life-long exploration of architecture in our time.

Therefore, in Chapter 3 we begin with an exploration of the role of *firmitas* in architecture. Vitruvius intended *firmitas* to include structural stability and the durability of the building's fabric. This continues to be a major part of what is required of a contemporary building. Of course, we all depend on our buildings to stand firm. But in our discussion of *firmitas* we will also emphasize the idea of firmness as it relates to buildings that endure over the years of changing uses and fashions. Our current tear-down, throw-away culture has led to the proliferation of buildings that are not expected to last more than a few decades.[5]

A huge amount of energy is embodied in the original materials and construction that undergo the demolition process, which is wasted as it is followed by the next round of material manufacture and construction. We are quickly realizing that this approach to building is simply not sustainable. This untenable situation suggests that an additional dimension to the concept of *firmitas* is needed, namely that a building be durable enough to safely accommodate many additions, reductions, and alterations over time. One term to describe this approach is *adaptive re-use.* It can sometimes require a redundancy, a generosity of strength that permits portions to be removed, or moved and altered, in order to fit a new use while avoiding the total tear-

---

[4] *Background buildings* is a term used by Paul Goldberger in his book *Why Architecture Matters*, Yale University Press, 2011. Goldberger defines these as the typical buildings that form the bulk of our environment, whose designs are perhaps adequate, but architecturally undistinguished.

[5] If a developer can depreciate a building over 20 years and extract adequate profit from its depreciation and rental during that period, he may feel that it is time to replace that structure with another one that fits changed needs, styles, and functions. Any residual structural quality in the teardown will only make the job harder.

down and replacement of an entire building. Related to this, we will assert that repairability is an essential aspect of a firm building. Because all buildings will continually age and decay, repairability equals longevity, postponing the need for replacement for as long as possible.

Chapter 4 will address Vitruvius's second concept, *utilitas* or usefulness, by which he meant meeting the needs of people by creating buildings that provide adequate protection from wind and rain, as well as plentiful access to light and ventilation, good drainage, and a workable arrangement of spaces for convenience and the production of needed goods. Today we have a much broader understanding of usefulness. It builds on Vitruvius's definition to include the encouragement of desired social interactions, the provision for modern needs for privacy and security, and affordability, not only of the initial cost of the facility but also the cost of heating and cooling the building over its lifetime. Today we expect a building not only to accommodate a long list of desired activities and uses but also to positively encourage and facilitate them.

We then re-examine *venustas* (which has been variously translated as beauty, delight, or aesthetic pleasure) in Chapter 5. In Vitruvius's time and place, *venustas* was guaranteed by following a set of rules governing proportions and motifs, particularly the orders of the columns: Doric, Ionic, or Corinthian. It is true that many of the ancient rules pertaining to proportion continue to be helpful in creating a pleasing and coherent result in which the parts echo the whole and vice versa. But here we will also update the notion of *venustas* to include not only the beauty of forms but also other related qualities that can generate interest, pleasurable memories, humor, intellectual challenge, and, when appropriate, even reflective sorrow (as in memorials). For us today a work of architecture may be beautiful or exciting, but we also hope to understand how it may offer pleasure in many other ways by being well integrated with its environment, instructive, harmonious, impressive, inspiring, thought-provoking, or thrilling.

Although there is some truth to the adage that beauty lies in the eye of the beholder, it is more true that visual pleasure is powerfully affected by proportion, variety, and order among the elements that we observe. Added to visual delight is physical pleasure, which can come from appropriate warmth and coolness, from comfortable movement through the building, and from the pleasant reverberation of sound. Then there is emotional satisfaction that arises from the ways the building offers possibilities for both graceful socialization and privacy. Finally, a building can offer intellectual delight by referring to ideas in a meaningful way, by instructing us about history or ritual, or by being humorous or even challenging. Architecture can offer pleasure by stimulating our interest in what we are seeing, feeling, and thinking as we use the building.

Many buildings, unfortunately, fall short of incorporating all three of Vitruvius's concepts. These three elements of architecture cannot be tacked on, as if some garnish of delight could be added to a building after it takes shape; they must emerge co-dependently and cooperatively during the design process. A building that is unbalanced in its incorporation of Vitruvius's triad may be firm and useful, but not particularly delightful. An amusement park structure may be useful and delightful, but is not particularly firm. A sculpture may be beautiful and firm, but arguably not useful. The act of making architecture is the attempt to combine all three of these elements successfully.

From our practice in the design of buildings, we have learned that the creation of a good building takes all three—firmness, usefulness, and aesthetic pleasure—into account simultaneously throughout the design process, from beginning to end. We know that good architecture isn't created by concocting a handsome form and then trying to cram the functions inside, or by asking a structural engineer to make the eccentric form "work" from a structural point of view. We know that the most successful examples of architecture grew naturally out of the three aims simultaneously.

It has been said that these three aspects are so interrelated that pure adherence to any two of them will guarantee the third, just as the growth of a tree demonstrates. As a tree matures, it develops additional woody material just where the trunk and branches are most stressed, and functional new branches and leaves appear as required by need and governed by DNA. Beauty emerges from this process naturally, automatically, as a result of life taking shape in response to the influences of its environment. The architectural critic Mariana van Rensselaer put it this way:

> Architectural beauty is not an extrinsic, superficial thing, depending on ornamental features, but is bound up with the very attainment of "firmness" and "commoditie." The really vital beauty of an architectural work consists in its clear expression of these two qualities.[6]

An apt symbol of this interrelationship between *firmitas, utilitas,* and *venustas* is the Borromeo knot, a set of three rings that are interrelated in a curious way: No two of the rings are connected to each other, yet all three comprise an inseparable knot, a unity. If any one of the three rings is removed, the entire group becomes separated. The unity depends on the presence of all three. As such, the Borromeo knot beautifully illustrates the necessity for all three of Vitruvius's virtues to be present: Without any one of them, the building fails to be fully "architectural."[7]

Among all the fine arts, architecture is unique: First, it must be

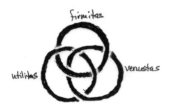

strong and functional as well as beautiful—none of the other fine arts are required to be useful (it is essential, in fact, that they *not* be useful so that their aesthetic mission can remain pure[8]); second, our

---

[6] Mariana van Rensselaer, "Recent Architecture in America," *Century,* May 1884, pp. 51-52.

[7] This analogy has been suggested by Donald Kunze at Penn State University in his article "The Vitruvian Virtues of Architecture: Utilitas, Firmitas, Venustas."

[8] The artist Richard Serra has put it this way: "Art is purposely useless . . . its significations are symbolic, internal, poetic . . . whereas architects have to answer to the program, the client, and everything that goes along with the utility function of the building. Let's not confuse the two things." Calvin Tomkins, *Lives of the Artists,* New York, Harry Holt and Co., 1980, p. 73.

experience of buildings and spaces is especially interactive in the physical sense. By visiting and inhabiting buildings, we make our mark on them, through the patina of use as well as the more willful modifications we make due to changing needs and sentiments. Musical scores do not change as they are performed or listened to repeatedly, nor do paintings or photographs respond to the repeated gazes of their owners or visitors. And works of literature, too, endure in their original form.

At the same time there is an important similarity between architecture and the other arts, namely that we can accept and enjoy many levels of mastery and significance. Just as we produce and enjoy our own untrained but enthusiastic singing and music-making and appreciate and support local pops and jazz groups, we also revere the masterworks of Bach, Beethoven, and Brahms. We don't define "music" solely as the work of our genius composers, but see it as a continuum from the personal and local to the expert and universal. The same can be said of the visual arts, literature, gastronomy, and architecture. All the arts are human productions: We can and do relate strongly to the whole spectrum of expression.

This is important to remember as we embark on our exploration of architecture. We are not just talking here about monuments—the Pyramids, Notre Dame Cathedral, Monticello—but the whole range of architectural works, from the indigenous structures of Africa, Asia, and the American Southwest to the current work of our most talented and well-known contemporary architects. In between these two extremes we will also consider the often rather ordinary design and building efforts that constitute 90 percent of our built environment: our individual homes and neighborhoods, our shopping centers of all sizes, our commercial and civic buildings, as well as our industrial and transportation facilities. What we will be exploring in this book is the notion that any of these design and building efforts is capable of achieving architectural merit to the extent that it successfully integrates the three "legs" of architecture: durability, utility, and beauty.

One might well ask, "Why all the emphasis on Vitruvius?" When one reads his writings today, it is a trip back to the 1st century B.C.E. in Rome. In his *Ten Books on Architecture* he specifies everything from how to choose a healthy site for a city to rules for the use of the ancient orders of Doric, Ionic, Corinthian—when they should be used and what their specific dimensions should be. His science was impressive for its time, but inadequate for today. There is a temptation to read some of his passages with amusement, recognizing how far we have advanced since Roman times. But his book's impact on the subsequent history of architecture is without equal. A forgotten copy of his book was discovered in the Swiss monastery of St. Gall in 1414, and the printing press was developed soon after, allowing his work to become available to a wide audience. Within a hundred years, translations were available in French and German. His basic ideas were then re-formulated by a succession of classically minded architectural theorists and practitioners during the Renaissance: Alberti, Serlio, and Palladio. The Vitruvian tradition of setting down architectural rules was thus carried forward, affecting not only the architecture of the Renaissance but also continuing in some real measure to the present time. Thomas Jefferson had several copies of Palladio's rulebook, and he used it to help him design (and redesign) his home, Monticello. Study of the clas-sical "orders" continued in American architectural schools through the early 20th century.

Besides the historical impact of Vitruvius's work, his very simple statement that buildings "must be built with due reference to durabil-ity, convenience, and beauty" has endured as a core concept, a jewel-like formulation, sitting innocently near the beginning of his book, and never specifically referred to again. Its very uniqueness lends it an aura of preciousness, like a nugget of gold embedded in a rock. It has proved to be the single most dependable criterion that architecture must meet. Other formulas that have attempted to define the qualities of architecture have tended to overemphasize one aspect or another, either beauty (John Ruskin in England in the 1840s), durability (most structural engineers of any age), or convenience (cranky critics, or indignant owners, who point out how poorly some buildings function). These various emphases are being reexamined today to see if they can be integrated into a more balanced approach. This attempt has been addressed in a recent article by Peter Buchanan, in which he proposes the restructuring of architectural education around the core areas of Vitruvius's firmness, commodity, and delight.[9]

In addition to this interest in rebalancing architectural education, some governmental agencies in both England and the United States have begun using the Vitruvian trio to more objectively evaluate the overall quality of new buildings. They have developed a "Design Quality Indicator" (DQI) to more realistically evaluate the new buildings they have commissioned. It views the trio as follows:

- Functionality (*utilitas*): the arrangement, quality, and interrelationship of spaces and how the building is designed to be useful to all.
- Build Quality (*firmitas*): the engineering performance of the building, which includes structural stability and the integration, safety, and robustness of the systems, finishes, and fittings.
- Impact (*venustas*): the building's ability to create a sense of place and have a positive effect on the local community and environment.

Finally, we propose to use this tripartite approach to organize our discussions in this book because we know that it has been at the heart of our own experience with buildings over the years, as well as that of the vast majority of all clients, builders, engineers, and architects, whether they profess it or not. Some may emphasize mainly the aesthetic aspect, others the role of problem solving, and yet others the technical and structural challenges. But the realization that all three considerations are at the heart of architecture will enable all of us—laypeople, professionals, and students—to approach the buildings around us with a deeper understanding and appreciation.

---

[9] Peter Buchanan, "The Big Rethink: Architectural Education," *The Architectural Review*, October 2012, p. 97. In addition to this triad, he adds "decorum," consisting of culture, history, and theory.

"If you wish to have a just notion of the magnitude of this city, you must not be satisfied with seeing its great streets and squares, but must survey the innumerable little lanes and courts. It is not in the showy evolutions of buildings, but in the multiplicity of human habitations which are crowded together, that the wonderful immensity of London consists."

—SAMUEL JOHNSON, FROM BOSWELL'S *THE LIFE OF SAMUEL JOHNSON*, 1763.

Awakening

ARCHIT

CHAPTER ONE

Awakening to
ARCHITECTURE

GIVEN THAT THE BUILT ENVIRONMENT SURROUNDING MOST OF us in our day-to-day lives can seem rather ordinary and not necessarily what one would think of as "architecture," it is surprising to us that so many people take a real interest in architecture. Yet, as architects, we are constantly meeting people with whom we share an enthusiasm and excitement about the built environment. These interests and enthusiasms take many forms: Some people follow news columns and websites written by architecture and urban design critics covering current design trends; some travel to visit architectural icons like the Pyramids or the Eiffel Tower or plan trips simply to experience the feeling and the culture of a city or place; some like to peruse the latest design periodicals; and several have had the experience of working with an architect on a project or attending a design review meeting for a proposed project at the urban planning offices in their own city.

These various levels of involvement show that people not only have a desire to learn more but also often want to be actively involved in the process of making architecture. In addition to their emotional and aesthetic responses to these different experiences, some develop a strong interest in architecture through their occupation or through a preference for a certain lifestyle. In recent years, many people have gotten more involved with the field because of a desire to have a positive impact on the environment. A few eventually go on to acquire the skills necessary to create architecture, first in school, then hopefully as participants in creating built environments, whether as practitioners or as clients.

Regardless of their ultimate level of engagement, many people come to have a strong feeling for architecture, bringing their enthusiasm, energy, and creativity into the mix. This first chapter, then, is for all of us, from the layperson to the student to the practitioner, who want to keep the flame of attention, awareness, and appreciation of architecture alive and bright. For some this will be entering new territory, for others it will be a revisiting of earlier experiences.

We'll consider several kinds of spatial experience through the lens of human development and explore the many and constantly evolving ways we relate to our environment as we mature. These are the ways, common to most of us, that we engage the essence of what architecture is before we may possess the tools to define it as such. Becoming more conscious of the innate tendencies that shape how we relate to our world can shed light on the roles our everyday surroundings can play in our lives. This recognition can then lead to a greater appreciation of the potential impacts of architecture as well as the many intentions behind it. Fundamentally, we don't need critics, expert knowledge, or trends to tell us what pleasures buildings and spaces offer. If we pay attention, we are all capable of recognizing these feelings as they arise from our own current and past experiences—whether we are sitting in an enclosed sunny garden, entering a magnificent concert hall, reading a book in a window alcove, or walking into a bustling city square.

As an aid to jogging our memories and focusing our attention, we'll start by following a loose chronology that begins with the qualities of our spatial experiences at birth, accompanies us through childhood, and then, finally, sends us out into the world to explore the significance of the structures and spaces of our everyday lives, our neighborhoods, our cities, and beyond.

SHELTER AND SAFETY

The first and most important source of an appreciation of architecture lies deep within us all, intrinsic in our biological "animalness" and submerged within layers of memory. This source is mostly subconscious, and it reflects how we may have related to our surroundings as small children and as we grew up. As adults, we often feel pleasure in the experience of true shelter and safety in a building, a sensation that we can connect with similar moments in childhood. This experience can include the pleasant feeling of being safe inside during a storm, or gathering together with others in a space made for that purpose, or in the simple satisfaction of owning a space that one has created for oneself. On the less pleasant side, most of us have also experienced disconcerting or fearful moments in relation to the spaces and places we inhabit. Feeling locked out or excluded when we are hoping for and perhaps needing unhindered access to a space can be a painful experience. The dark basement or attic can also seem like a forbidding and frightening place when we are young, the source of scary monster stories or ghostly figures from the past.

When we recall our childhood contentedness with space and place, we can then naturally apply it to similar spaces and places around us now. These memories serve as inner rudders and signposts leading us to make genuine responses to the environments we currently inhabit.

We all depend on these early memories (both satisfying and sometimes disconcerting) to help shape our later reactions to the buildings around us. It starts in early childhood with our physical need for shelter and safety. Beginning at birth, with the loss of the protecting womb and the abrupt shock of open space and cold, we stop crying only when we are physically re-embraced, warmed, snugly wrapped in a blanket. For the rest of our lives our natural tendency is to seek physical enclosure strong and solid enough to contain and protect us. This search drives many of our choices relating to how we inhabit spaces. These spaces include those at all dimensions of scale—from our bed, to our house, to our city.

A stone park shelter embodies the feel of a rugged, sturdy structure, offering secure contrast with the natural outdoors it serves.[1]

Young children often satisfy and express this need for shelter and safety through constructive play by draping sheets over tables and chairs, thereby creating delightful child-sized enclosures. This activity is very powerful for the child because he or she is actively creating, or designing, the small-scale space that is so vividly felt as satisfying. The architect Karen Fiene filled her entire living room with such a structure when she was a child, with her parents' apparent blessing. She created the "memory drawing" (below), adding the following comment: "The view . . . a feeling of being in a soft warm cave . . . very private and safe, totally invisible. One peeks out through a keyhole. Translucent light filters through the blankets . . . a yellow one is best."

---

[1] This 1930s WPA-built Shelter #7 is in Wyandotte County Lake Park, Kansas City, Kansas.

SOCIAL INTERACTION AND TOGETHERNESS

Our human need to bond with others most often takes place in architectural space after we begin to walk, perhaps in front of the family fireplace, at the kitchen table, or on the patio. Our experience of inhabiting such spaces along with other people resonates with a sense of wholeness, a specificity that is easily remembered. Our memories of these spaces are united with the emotional bonding that took place within them. Later in life, when we encounter a similar fireplace, kitchen table, or patio, the memories and emotions of our earliest relationships are often called up in response. When we encounter a new fireplace hearth, we subconsciously gauge whether we can sit close enough to see, hear, and talk to one another (but not too close) while also sharing in the warmth and brightness of the fire. Can we find a comfortable place to sit or stand nearby? Will the space allow for a sufficient enclosure for our group, concentrating our conversation within the embracing warmth of the fire? In this sense, the fire circle encourages social togetherness, as well as a physical and emotional sense of personal security and protection.

An unhappy family life can also be linked in our memory to the places that contained it. The 2009 German film *The White Ribbon*

portrays an example of bitter punishment of children that takes place at the dining table, and the resulting permanent psychological damage. For those children, any dining table will certainly echo with this pain.

As we mature, our social bonding takes place in ever larger and more public spaces. As teens, our schools, summer camps, and larger gathering and assembly spaces can be the important locales where our social bonding takes place. For others, the bonding will occur in streets or woods. In later years, when we return to a school or camp as adults, we see it partly through the eyes of our youth, charging what we see in the environment with the intense emotions that permeate our memories of the times we had there (for good or ill). Similarly, our current experience of a city we are revisiting will be sharpened as we recall details from our first visit there. A few hours spent in a cozy cafe on a rainy day will give rise to some of the same emotions that flowed through us as children, when the family gathered around the dinner table during a storm.

PLACES OF ADVANTAGE

Not only do we long for security and protection, we also require access to the great beyond; although we have a desire to be contained by the spatial experience of "In," we also need the complementary sense of the expansive "Out." As children, we discover the pleasure and fun of locating ourselves in a position of overlook, giving us a sense of advantage, a special spot where we can see and hear others but they aren't aware of us. We're hiding, but in such a way that we are able to spy on the rest of the world. In a two-story house, we may lie down next to the upper floor's railing and peer over, down into the living room below, where the adult action is going on, secretly watching and listening.

The pleasure we get from this position of advantage lies deep within our animal nature. Like lions crouching on a limb to better surprise prey below or simply to rest in a position of safety and advantage, our ancestors sought out high, protected places from which to apprehend approaching danger and to have a height advantage to either attack or defend. The vestigial pleasure we now experience is some combination of feeling comfortably safe and strong and maintaining our ability to access the world beyond, both physically and by sight. As spying chil-

dren, we are intensely curious, feeling a bit superior to those below, and are hugely entertained by our advantaged position.

Overlooks of all kinds give us the same grown-up pleasure. The distant scenic view from peaks and hilltops, the window view down into the street, and the view from the balcony down into the courtyard and rooms below are all positions of prospect that are exciting, interesting, and fun.

These situations of overlook, or prospect, are examples of spaces that reassure us that we can escape without undue notice—an important kind of freedom that some spaces can offer us. As adults, we remember the pleasure of having the option to leave, escape, and move out into the world beyond. This dialogue between In and Out is one of the fundamental aspects of the environment that we respond to. We will instinctively respond favorably to a space that offers both possibilities, whereas we might have a degree of anxiety in a space that has no obvious exit or connection with the outdoors. Our awakening to architecture can include paying attention to whether a room or building (or city) balances the visual opportunities for easy movement from inside to outside, and vice versa, depending on our mood at the time.

PROSPECT AND OWNERSHIP

Children soon develop a sense of what is theirs, what belongs to them, and what they wish belonged to them. First a toy, then a room, perhaps even the house. A hand-drawn sign will sometimes appear, posted on a door to a room announcing to whom it belongs, as well as who is welcome in that room and who isn't.

Did you have a tree house as a child, or dream of having one? Such an experience can forever change one's sensitivity to the power of man-made spaces. The tree house combines several pleasures—a locale for social togetherness (a club), prospect over the surrounding world to ensure privacy and control of access, and ownership of one's own space—along with the right to include or exclude anyone you wish. Such an exclusive perch facilitates great adventuring, both real and imagined, that often involves plotting against enemies or cooking up delicious mischief. It can provide the perfect clubhouse, cementing relationships while nurturing confidence and new skills.

The front porch can be our semi-private clubhouse, up from the yard and street a bit, a good place for dreaming, planning, and sharing.

We carry this early image of environmental pleasure with us internally as we mature, ready to respond positively when we encounter echoes of this early structure in our current buildings. Any place that combines overlook, some effort or difficulty of access, and a measure of exclusivity invites a welling up of earlier remembered pleasures. A hilltop cafe reached by stone steps, a private residence settled into the hills amongst the trees, or a private room with views down through trees to the activities below are examples of such potentially pleasurable places that resonate with our earliest experiences of privileged ownership. One archetypal form of space that combines many of these elements is the front porch of a house or stoop of a building, elevated a bit over the sidewalk and street below, with comfortable chairs or steps that invite us to sit and observe whatever passes by. Even if we are renting, this posture summarizes and recapitulates our early experience of ownership, exclusivity, and prospect.

THE PLEASURE OF
SHAPING AND MAKING

Architecture consists of buildings that have been designed and assembled with thought, planning, and skill. And as we grow up, many of us experience a basic need to be able to successfully organize and shape the world around us using our thinking, planning, and other developing skills. At a very young age this might take the form of putting blocks together and taking them apart, creating small worlds from the results of each kind of assembly. As a child in the early 1870s, architect Frank Lloyd Wright played with wooden building blocks developed by German educationalist Friedrich Froebel to stimulate children's conceptual and manual dexterity skills. Wright later said this experience was instrumental in the development of his spatial and organizational sense.

Other forms of childhood shaping can vary from organizing one's own room, to conceiving and building toys (usually models of "real" objects), to mastering the ability to draw. When we like something that we have thus made, we are proud of it and typically display it. The liberating aspect of children's shaping is that it is endlessly transformative, changeable, and risk-free. If we don't like it, we can rip it apart and start over with something else.

The pleasure that we find in our youthful creations lays the groundwork for later enjoyment of beautiful things. It prepares us to notice and then appreciate well-conceived and well-built objects of all kinds—*objets d'art*, vehicles, furniture, electronic devices . . . and buildings.

PLAYING WITH SCALE

Dollhouses are interesting examples of children modeling an imaginary world for themselves, working with the fixed conditions of the house itself and endlessly rearranging, refurnishing, and acting out activities that might occur within. In 1962, Mattel® came out with a very popular cardboard "Barbie's® Dream House," with a full set of

furniture and other furnishings that could be arranged and rearranged to explore alternate room layouts.

One of the interesting aspects of dollhouses is that the child is given a certain amount of initial order and structure. Usually the house and furniture are given, and the child arranges these pieces in pleasing ways. Each arrangement takes on a kind of reality, a believable place that the child can fill with imaginary people and actions. Creating these small-scale versions of places, spaces, and things exercises the mental skills of attention, imagination, creativity, and intelligence, allowing them to grow and develop.

The modeling of "working" vehicles and structures is another exciting pleasure for many children. One of the simplest, and perhaps earliest, examples is the erection of a house of playing cards. Each individual card stands by leaning up against its neighbors, and the walls of the first story are roofed by flat cards on top, which then form the base for successive levels. The placement of each card takes lots of skill and care, as well as insight about how it can add to the overall structure.

But what is so exquisitely pleasurable (and eventually painful) is the precariousness of the growing structure as it gets larger and higher. The structure must "work," that is, it must stand—resisting both gravity and any slight air movements that strike it. Eventually, someone will sneeze or bump the table, and the house of cards will collapse with a suddenness that brings both tears and shouts of joy. The art and science of assembly comes up against the environmental forces of gravity, wind, and "earthquake," creating an early opportunity to participate in the same basic processes and interactions that go into the creation of architecture.

The other important aspect of model-making is that it requires manual dexterity and control, mastery of the acts of cutting, sanding, and attaching, all while using tools and trying not to injure oneself. Above all, the child who attempts to create a model of a house, car, or plane will of necessity develop patience—lots of it. But success in this activity of model-making will result in a sense of accomplishment that brings great pleasure and self-satisfaction. Children who develop a taste for making models will appreciate well-formed and well-conceived objects—like architecture—for the rest of their lives.[2]

The more advanced and complex model-making that is involved in creating model trains, cars, and airplanes requires that these models be both strong enough to withstand their eventual operation and functional enough to actually chug around the track, roll down the road, or fly through the air with all their parts intact and without crashing. The modeler who succeeds will likely take great satisfaction in seeing his or her creation doing what it was designed to do.

When young people design and build models of vehicles, rooms, and cities, they are tapping into another very human source of pleasure, that of delight in the tiny, the miniature, the smaller than real life.[3] Little cars and little play kitchens put us in control of these imaginary things and places long before we are ready to use them in real life. This form of play allows us to invent, enter, and participate in whole worlds through imagination, sometimes in energetic collaboration with fellow playmates and sometimes as solitary adventurers. Creating small versions of things or places can also give us a preview of the adult relationships to things and places that we will eventually attain. They can even help us to explore personal issues or relationships by creating safe worlds in which to confront and engage with potentially difficult emotions or situations, as is the goal of some art therapy techniques.

On the other hand, we also instinctively find delight in the gigantic, overscaled object, as the artist Claes Oldenburg demonstrates with his huge sculptures of a clothes pin, a bow and arrow, or a cherry in a spoon.

---

[2] To state the obvious, young people today spend less time with creative play, spending more with TV, computers, and smartphones. This passivity likely impairs a student's readiness for the form and space-making aspect of architectural design.

[3] Fantastic miniature period rooms at a scale of one inch to the foot can be seen at the Chicago Art Institute.

"Spoonbridge and Cherry" by sculptors Claes Oldenburg and Coosje Van Bruggen at the Walker Art Center in Minneapolis, Minnesota.

Our early delight in playful changes of scale can serve us well as we later develop an interest in architecture. We then see that architectural elements—doors, ceiling heights, and street widths—are all manipulable and can be selected to fit, or contrast with, our bodies. But we never lose our awe of really big, big things.

EXPLORING NEW PLACES RIGHT WHERE YOU LIVE

A good place to begin an exploration of architecture is to spend some time in the unexplored parts of the town where you live. Experiencing the buildings of a new environment can be a powerful way to ignite and grow an interest in architecture. There are typically many unexplored parts of your hometown that can open your eyes to unique and fascinating buildings.

An early assignment for us when we began our architectural studies in the late 1960s was to explore and report on a neighborhood that we were unfamiliar with. Our group selected the Nihonmachi, or Japantown area, of San Francisco for our project. We walked along with camera and sketchpad to observe and record the shops and residences along the street, really looking for the first time at an environment that we had formerly simply driven past. Overcoming our original shyness of asking questions of the residents, we decided to look into an old synagogue that had been made into a Zen Buddhist Center.

THE APPEAL OF THE BIG

The childlike awe and delight in the giant, the super-scaled—a mixture of excitement, admiration, and a little fear—stays with us as adults. We attempt to comprehend the stunning hugeness of monuments like the Pyramids or the unprecedented height of the latest high-rises around the world. When first-year students of architecture are asked to submit a favorite building, they will often select something from the "bigness" category. For example, the Burj Khalifa building in Dubai, completed in 2009, is currently the tallest existing building at around one-half mile in height.

Bigness in itself is fascinating because of its scale in reference to ourselves: When we meditate upon the massive amounts of design, material, and construction effort that are embodied in the building, deeper levels of awe and amazement result, and our appreciation for the existence of such an accomplishment grows.

Great Pyramid at Giza (150 meters high); Empire State Building (400 meters); the Burj Khalifa (800+ meters)

Sokoji Soto Zen Temple, Japantown (Nihonmachi), San Francisco

We were welcomed in and invited to join a sitting group of Zen students with the assurance that lunch would soon be served. After the calm sitting, and a simple bowl of veggies for lunch, we thanked our hosts and left, only later realizing that we had inadvertently stumbled upon a gathering led by the newly arrived Japanese teacher Suzuki Roshi, a group that would soon become the San Francisco Zen Center. Many years later, purely coincidentally, they would become one of our clients.

Later on that same day, we knocked on the front door of a very impressive Victorian house in the neighborhood and met Gavin Chester Arthur, who we then learned was a flamboyant gay liberation leader, leader of a commune, and grandson of President Chester Arthur.

What did we learn about architecture that day? Nothing specifically about how to create it, but rather that a neighborhood could be amazingly diverse and rich, that older buildings are capable of cheerfully accepting a new use and clientele, and that a small group of students with a camera and sketch pad can knock and open some interesting doors. Buildings can accommodate and support a variety of human activities even if they were originally designed for another activity. This experience sparked our interest in how neighborhoods and buildings function for people.

FINDING ARCHITECTURE IN THE BUILDINGS AROUND US

One barrier to the appreciation of architecture is that a good portion of our environment consists of simply uninteresting buildings. Examples include big box stores and strip malls, each the same, with very minor variation from location to location. Another barrier is the opposite, the structures and streetscapes that make a desperate attempt to stand out in order to grab our attention. The experience of driving for miles along a strip-mall street consisting of a series of one-story stores, each shouting out a different design image or wild sign, can be so jarring that once the initial shock wanes, our senses become deadened to the cacophony.

But if we explore a bit we'll find, fortunately, that these aren't the whole story. Scattered amongst the neighborhoods of identical rows of houses and the unsettling visual ricochet of strip-mall structures and signage we can usually spot some delightful exceptions. Within our towns and neighborhoods are some earlier buildings, original farmhouses, older post offices, banks, and libraries that were originally built well enough to have survived the passing decades. These survivors have occasionally been converted to new uses, and they often attract our attention due to their history, textures, and forms, and their unique qual-

Berkeley Main Post Office, designed by Oscar Wenderoth in 1914

Berkeley High School expansion, by ELS Architecture and Urban Design, 2001

ities of design and patina of age. The public will often become involved in preserving these older structures that offer historical interest and a concrete link with the past. For example, many cities are graced with interesting libraries and post office buildings. The design of the post office shown on the facing page, for instance, was based on Brunelleschi's hospital for abandoned children in Florence, begun in 1419.

In every town and neighborhood there also will be a few examples of brand new buildings that intend to be more thoughtful, innovative, and meaningful than typical. For example, directly across the street from this post office sits a high school, with its bold and dramatic recent addition, executed in a modern streamlined way that harmonizes with the original Moderne building without copying it.

These more provocative buildings will be produced by enlightened clients, builders, and designers who share a love of "architecture." The buildings will stand out from their neighbors, stretching the bounds of general expectation and acceptability, usually by being bolder in their concept and execution, with a larger or deeper connection to the client, the user, and the passing public. Above all, they will be interesting and will capture the attention of the neighbors and those who pass by.

In spite of the occasional good building in our neighborhoods, their infrequency can be one of the biggest barriers to becoming interested in architecture. Those of us who live in older, historic cities will often have more significant and interesting buildings close at hand, whereas those in relatively young cities and neighborhoods might find that buildings worthy of more architectural interest are fewer and farther between. If our general culture is not deeply and intensely concerned with and appreciative of architecture, it isn't because of a lack of sensitivity to the environment. Indeed, many sensitive people will of necessity, as a matter of aesthetic survival, avert their eyes and attention. They may mentally and visually insulate themselves from both the potentially overwhelming presence of insipid and uninspiring structures and the buildings that simply attempt to attract attention by loud colors or extravagant but meaningless gestures of design.

But those who nurture an ongoing interest in architecture, be they laypeople, critics, architects, or teachers of architecture, recognize the potential pleasure afforded by an appreciation for the occasionally delightful qualities of a few buildings. As our enthusiasm and knowledge develop, we open up to the pleasures offered by architecture (and food, and art, and music), and we are more likely to also find beauty in the everyday, the apparently ordinary and less significant examples that surround us wherever we go. We can become more aware of the small, partial, and occasional elements within the less remarkable examples that can also offer pleasurable qualities. The cuisine enthusiast enjoys the wares proffered by a street vendor selling hot dogs once in a while, not because the simple fare represents any elevation of the art, but because it provides a sense of relaxation, an acceptance of and pleasure in the spontaneous, the available, and the unpretentious. Similarly, a gas station can give comfort and reassurance on a long road trip, not because of its architectural merit, but precisely because of its familiarity and guarantee of certain services and comforts.

This pleasure in the habitual is most vividly experienced when traveling in a foreign country, when the familiar cash machine or menu gives us a temporary reprieve from the unrelenting strangeness of the new. Artists, musicians, gourmands, and architects periodically find inspiration by tapping into the ordinary and the "unholy" in order to reconnect with the predominant culture and to reorient their main focus and enthusiasm. This relevance of the ordinary in architecture was first pointed out very effectively by Robert Venturi and Denise Scott Brown in the early 1970s, looking at the built culture of Las Vegas, even taking their University of Pennsylvania students there for architectural field trips.[4]

---

[4] Venturi, Izenour, and Scott Brown, *Learning from Las Vegas*, MIT Press, 1972.

THE POSSIBILITIES OF TRAVEL

When we travel to a new place our perceptual antennae are sharpened and resensitized—our eyes, ears, nose, mouth, skin, and muscles all take in fresh images and sensations. We notice everything in a new, more observant way. Our general level of energy goes up as we prepare ourselves to deal with all this new information. We take greater interest in everything that surrounds us, and that includes the architecture.

Research has shown that people who eventually get involved in architecture were often children in families that moved from city to city as they grew up. This makes some intuitive sense in that a child on the move experiences many alternate homes and neighborhoods, each of which requires new mental mapping of the environment: the house arrangement, the location of friends in the neighborhood, the location of the school and playground. The required remapping attunes and develops that part of the brain that deals with relationships in space, an important skill for understanding buildings and neighborhoods.

Travel gives us all a chance to try out new ways of seeing and acting. Those who normally drive the three blocks to the grocery at home will happily walk for blocks and miles in a new town, enjoying the fresh and different buildings and streets. (As an aside, it's interesting once in a while to walk a route that you usually drive; it's amazing what you see that you miss from the car.) This is equally true of new cultures—new food and dress and manners. Upon returning home, the memories will be accessible, adding to our store of possible building types, construction, scale, and colors.

Experiencing the variety of design in the world away from home permits us to encounter buildings with a richer background of design ideas and patterns. It broadens our readiness to experience more places in a deeper, more explorative manner. We've had the experience of returning home after a trip and recognizing that many elements of familiar buildings around us may have been influenced by the buildings we've just seen on our travels: the bold contrasting colors we saw in Mexico, a garden bridge over a pond that reminds us of one we saw in Japan, or a steep roof with deep overhangs similar to a Scandinavian barn.

IDEALISM AND SOCIAL RESPONSIBILITY

Have you ever looked at or been in a building and said to yourself, "I don't know anything about architecture, but I think I could do a better job than that"? The feeling that, given a chance, we have the simple good sense and sensibility to improve some part of the environment can be the spark that ignites a passion for architecture.

Homelessness is a real problem in today's cities, and it is hard not to wonder about how straightforward it would be to design and fabricate simple economic shelters, structures that would provide badly needed protection from the weather and a bit of security. For some, reading in the newspapers about widespread poverty and nonexisting or minimal housing can encourage them to pursue a career in one of the service professions: medicine, social work, or perhaps architecture. Many architects choose to work toward affordable housing for the poor through organizations such as Habitat for Humanity. Others contribute to emergency housing following natural disasters and development projects in the Third World through organizations like Architecture for Humanity.

The architect Shigeru Ban, for example, has made a specialty of work in emergency housing and community services throughout the

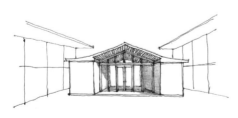 world, trying to use readily available materials. Following the 2011 earthquake and tsunami in Japan, he designed and helped install emergency privacy shelters for families taking refuge in a gymnasium,

using rolled paper tubes for structure and hung canvases for walls. He followed this with new temporary housing and a central community center using surplus shipping containers (facing page).

A group that can greatly benefit from socially responsible architecture is aging Americans, who of necessity are increasingly demanding accessible buildings that provide delightful, sunlit spaces for living and socializing as well as for quiet personal time. Accessibility, or Universal Design, includes the careful selection of appliances and amenities and the design of easily accessible objects and elements, especially when aging is accompanied by serious disabilities. Talk to an architect who has designed an affordable and accessible housing complex and received appreciation from the tenants and you will get a sense of how rewarding this type of work can be.

The planning of our cities and their growth patterns also needs to be reconsidered. The ever-expanding outward growth of urban areas takes up too much rural agricultural land and depends too much upon the automobile, all of which simply isn't sustainable. This is primarily a task for urban planners and designers, but architects can play an important role in the design of more sustainable cities.

There is also the ever present need for well-designed, energy-efficient housing for the general population. Thus, an interest in "saving the world" through sustainability can easily lead to an interest in architecture. The energy embodied in the physical creation of our buildings, and more critically, their ongoing energy use for lighting, heating, and cooling, comprises the major proportion of our country's energy demand. If we want to make our earth sustainable, we need to transform the design of our cities and buildings. Today, much of the interest in architecture stems from a concern with creating buildings that conserve energy and resources, that don't pollute the air, or whose materials of construction don't cause allergies and longer-term illness. These concerns are finally becoming part of the basis of well-designed buildings and are inspiring a new generation to take a fresh look at the role of architecture in making a better world.

TALK TO AN ARCHITECT

People who are starting to get interested in architecture sometimes attribute that interest to the influence of a relative or close friend who happens to be an architect or works in a related profession—landscape architect, contractor, interior designer, or developer. Sometimes you might receive support from one of these professionals who will pin hopes on you, encouraging you to take up some work related to design. Alternatively, they just might try to dissuade you, citing the inevitable difficulties of the profession: getting work, making money, avoiding lawsuits, receiving appropriate credit for one's contribution. But in spite of learning about the downsides, spending time with someone who is enthusiastically practicing a design skill can be a powerful incentive to exploring design further.

What is it that they enjoy? If they are having a good time practicing design, maybe you could too. Some of the attractive aspects that practitioners talk about include the pleasures of creatively working out a problem, exploring spatial ideas using the tools of drawing and erasing, building models, presenting solutions to colleagues and clients, being able to respond to helpful feedback from them, interacting with consultants, getting final approval on plans, periodically observing and contributing to the construction process, and receiving praise and thanks for doing such a good job. A sense of creativity, satisfaction, status—these can seem very attractive and spark a real interest in an architectural career.

Relatives and friends may also have some insight into your personality and skills that you may not yet perceive. You might learn that you have some important developing characteristics that could help you in a design career. These might include interest in people, intelligence, curiosity, and an aesthetic sensibility. Hearing this might encourage your interest in architecture—and it should.

WATCHING BUILDINGS
GO UP AND COME DOWN

It is surprising to notice that a familiar building is gone, and fascinating to see one being demolished. Some wooden buildings come down with just a few crunches, whereas reinforced concrete buildings take a lot of powerful machinery, energy, and time. Those of us who are sensitive to the issue of sustainability may take a sense of satisfaction in just how difficult it is to claw down a well-built building, wondering if it would have been better to remodel than to replace.

But a special fascination accompanies the rise of a new building. Even if we have to peer through observation holes in the surrounding barrier wall, we can't resist keeping periodic tabs on the construction progress. Watching a new building come to life, or being a member of the construction crew, can generate an interest in architecture. Here, we'd each like to share a formative experience. First Shelley:

> While a student living in New York City, I was walking down a familiar street one morning and saw something, or perhaps it would be better to say I felt something, that helped me be more aware of the impact architecture could have. It was a street that I had walked down many times, but this time it felt different. It was hard to say exactly what had changed; the street felt much sunnier than usual and also a little quieter. The sounds had shifted too, somehow. After a moment I realized that a five-story building on the south side of the street had disappeared, opening up a wide swath of space all the way over to 22nd Street. The entire building had been completely demolished within just a few days, pulled away from the building next to it, leaving behind a few brick piles in a vacant lot and a new light-filled, airy space in the middle of the block; it seemed as though a giant tooth had been plucked out of the jaw of the street.
>
> It was a recognition of a sudden change in the environment that made me realize I was carrying impressions of many streets and places I knew in the city, though unconsciously, and that the perception of a change came through all my senses before I was able to actually identify what it was. It struck me that we are probably doing this more often than we realize:

Looking south across 23rd Street in New York City, through an empty space where a building had existed just weeks before.

Before we come up with concepts about the things and places that make up our environment, we feel them first, in our bodies, and we hold on to these detailed impressions wordlessly, often for a long time.

In addition to the street's new sense of space and sound, the building had left some interesting traces behind, some partial remnants of its former life. Still attached to the wall of the next-door building were strips of wood where the floors and walls of old rooms used to be. Some patches of old wall were covered with bathroom tile, some with flowered wallpaper, some with faded wood paneling. Here and there, a flat diagonal strip zigzagged up or down. Stairs! And there was someone's bathroom and there had been someone's closet. These marks of former spaces left a profound effect on me. What had first seemed just an empty space came alive with possibility, and with the memories of coming and going over the years and the hidden intimate lives of people.

Now Max:

In 1948 my folks commissioned a new, modest house in the remote outskirts of Denver. Every weekend we would drive far out to the edge of civilization, out in the barren fields of weeds and rabbits, to watch the building grow up and out of the ground. I watched the work, but didn't really comprehend that I would live there someday. To tell the truth, a house under construction isn't very appealing yet as a domicile—it's cold, dark, full of dirt and construction debris. It felt like it took forever to finish. Even though the walls were going up, I still didn't believe we would actually live there.

But one day we went to the new house and spent our first night in it. We ate dinner and sat around a fire in the new fireplace; I slept in my bed in my new bedroom. In one night, that construction site we had visited on Sundays became my home. Perhaps that was the real beginning of my interest in architecture. From then on, whenever I see a new building under construction I understand that it will eventually become a home, an office, or a factory for someone's real life.

"The building became our home as soon as we started to live in it."

THE UNFORGETTABLE IMPACT OF A GREAT BUILDING OR PLACE

Some of us will have the experience of encountering a city, neighborhood, or building that simply stuns us with architectural impact. This experience may completely redirect our feeling for the positive potential of a wonderful physical environment, establishing a lifelong appreciation for the craft of design and building. The particular place or environment might range from a native village in Mexico to a Roman temple in Italy, or from a Parisian corner cafe to a great modern sports arena.

The places that have affected us profoundly were not all designed by architects, and are not all famous. What is significant is the impact they had on us as we walked through their spaces, used them, made contact with their materials of construction, and contemplated their aesthetic, symbolic, and intellectual effects upon us. They lit an inner fire of enthusiasm and passion for buildings that has sustained us through the years.

Old Faithful Inn at Yellowstone National Park, Wyoming, R.C. Reamer, 1904.

A few of the sites and buildings that have proved central to our awakening to architecture are the indigenous hill towns of Italy, the huge rural barns throughout America, the city of Paris and the buildings of New York (especially Grand Central Station), gothic churches in France, Pueblo and Spanish buildings made of adobe brick in New Mexico, the magnificent lodges of our national parks (like Old Faithful Inn[5] in Yellowstone), and most of the buildings by our hometown hero architect, Bernard Maybeck, especially his Christian Science Church.

A more detailed example of a great building that has influenced us is Palladio's Villa Emo of 1559 in the little town of Fanzolo north of Venice. Many years ago, we (Max and his wife Helen) made a pilgrimage of Palladio's villas, searching each one out in the countryside. Of the many wonderful villas we visited, Emo struck us with the most profound and lasting impact. Instead of the typical country farmsteads we passed on the way, with their informal cluster of main house, farm accessories, and towers, all built of yellow and terra-cotta brick, Villa Emo's first surprise was its symmetrical, linear white-stuccoed form, long and straight, stretched out tautly across the landscape, defining a broad front yard and an 80-acre pasture and orchard in the rear. Crossing at the center of the villa is a second major axis consisting of the main entry path, flanked by rows of poplar trees, leading directly to the front and back

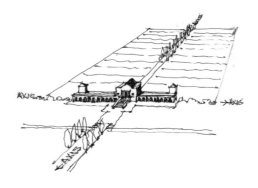

[5] Old Faithful Inn was designed by 29-year-old architect Robert Charles Reamer. It was built of lodgepole pine in 1904, and is a National Historic Landmark. Its great room is anchored by a massive stone four-sided fireplace, surrounded by a spider-web of stairways and balconies, all made of natural pine branches. Like all great lodges, it reflects the vastness and power of the national park with its great volume built with raw materials from the site. It feels as if it were constructed by a heroic race of playful giants.

entries. These twin axes meet at the center of the house and make a powerful statement: This land and its building constitute a single entity, a formal partnership of productive land and the structure that will help to manage it, and when you are related to these axes, you are a part of this factory/farm too.

The plan is simple and totally functional. The four-story cube at the center contains the house/managerial headquarters. Reaching out to either side are identical lower farm facilities for the animals, equipment, produce storage, and workspaces. Taller dovecot towers terminate each arm. All the levels connect with each other so that all the farm operations can be supervised by the owner, moving from the main house under cover, protected from rain and summer sun (similar to a New England connected farm building that permits access protected from deep snows). Here is Palladio's plan and elevation, published after construction in his *Four Books of Architecture* in 1570.

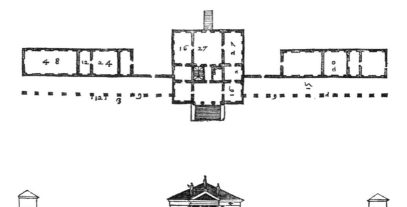

Palladio's plan and elevation of Villa Emo illustrates how the whole building operates as both a house for the owner and a factory farmhouse. (From Palladio's *The Four Books of Architecture*, 1570)

So what is so deeply moving about Villa Emo? First, in spite of the temple-like composition of the facade, construction is of local brick, not stone, but the brick is then covered with white stucco, smoothing and simplifying the exterior surface. Structurally, it is modest, conservative, and affordable. It has stood up well for over 450 years; it is firm. Next, it is supremely functional. It is a factory farmhouse, designed primarily to grow the corn recently imported from the New World (replacing the less nutritious millet) for the sustenance of the peasants who grew it on leased land and for the profit of the landowners from their portion. And it was functional in the sense that it provided a comfortable summer getaway for the owners, far from the heat (and plague) of the city.

Finally, the villa elicited a deep aesthetic response in us, and a surprising one: Instead of rustic charm and the relaxed informality of natural materials, warm colors, and soft contours, we found an exciting freshness and energy that emerged from the crisp elegance of the buildings. We experienced a welcome change of coolness and spareness, an honest stripping away of the unnecessary. And that clarity of form and surface enabled us to recognize the sophisticated underlying geometry, the well-proportioned surfaces on the exterior as well as of the room plans and heights. Each of the rooms in the main building, for instance, lies within a grid and has a good length to width proportion, and all the rooms are interrelated by sharing dimensions—they fit comfortably to each other, the large to the moderate to the small. Each part plays an essential role in the whole.

Our Palladian odyssey, especially to the Villa Emo, made a deep impression on us, and led to a later study and appreciation for classical proportioning systems and the role of the country villa in the life of 16th-century Italians. It also revealed certain parallels between Palladio's villas and country commissions that we architects would get in later years.

As a student, Shelley had a similar Italian experience in Verona, a town in northern Italy:

A friend had suggested I visit the Castelvecchio (The Old Castle) Museum,[6] saying that a well-known local architect, Carlo Scarpa, had completed the redesign of the old castle into a museum about ten years before. I planned to spend a few hours there, but ended up staying the whole day.

As the afternoon went on, the light changed and the feel of the spaces changed with it: They felt different than in the morning; they were filled with new shadows and sounds. The architect had carefully planned these changing light qualities in response to the qualities of the original 14th-century structures. He had transformed them into comfortable and pleasing spaces, both inviting to visitors while still retaining the qualities of an ancient dwelling. By placing a new layer of materials like blackened steel and light marble into the passageways, stairs, and old castle rooms, Scarpa had created a new clarity in the way each space led to the next. This new layer of elements placed inside the old walls set up the medieval icons and statues to be viewed in a new way, and it was just as valid and important as the original building; he had come up with a new organization of the spaces and the way people moved through them, while still preserving the rough old brick and stone walls.

---

[6] The sketch is a view of the space between two wings of the Castelvecchio. The two wings are linked by a suspended walkway constructed of steel and wood, designed by Carlo Scarpa in the 1960s. As you cross the walkway, you are given dynamic views of the 14th-century equestrian statue of the castle's original builder, Lord Cangrande II della Scala, perpetually ready for battle and keeping an eye on his city from his perch high above the ground.

Admittedly, the capacity to be deeply impressed by architecture is perhaps enabled by some preparation: the experience of other good places, a bit of knowledge about the specific place, and maybe some attempts to design buildings in school. It is thrilling to come upon a building that you previously studied in a history class. The inner fire referred to earlier is an apt metaphor for an enthusiasm for architecture, one that can start with the kindling of childhood play in space, be gradually built up with some later education, and be brought into full flame by experiencing deeply moving places.

FASHION: WHAT'S HOT AND WHAT'S NOT

So far we have been talking about how your own experience can give rise to an interest in architecture. But awareness of architecture is often sparked by the most recent or most unusual new building projects that are in the news. We are talking here about the general tendency of people to be fascinated with The New, the most recent building design (or hairstyle or shoe shape) to hit the scene. A recent building will be featured in the media, and the mere newness and originality of the project's form will kindle interest. A new building often captures our attention because it looks different than the buildings we are used to and because it affects its surroundings and changes the quality of its neighborhood, for better or worse. The new building may represent novel ideas about how a building should be structured, organized, or simply look. And its designer may have some thought-provoking things to say about the new work that might open our eyes to the many ways architecture impacts our lives. For example, Daniel Libeskind, a designer at the forefront of contemporary architecture who created the winning plan for the reconstruction of the World Trade Center, recently completed a new addition to the Military History Museum in Dresden, Germany.

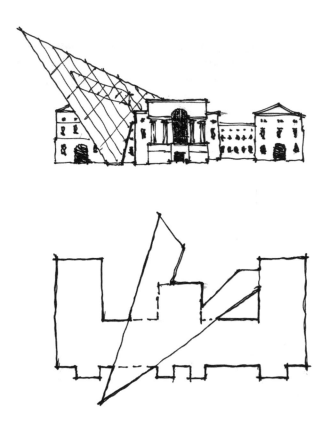

Diagrammatic plan and elevation sketches of Libeskind's Military History Museum in Dresden, Germany, completed in October 2011.

He says of this very radical design, "I wanted to create a bold interruption, a fundamental dislocation, to penetrate the historic arsenal." And so he did. The description of the addition that appears on his firm's website continues:

> Libeskind's winning design boldly interrupts the original building's symmetry. The extension, a massive, five-story 14,500-ton wedge of concrete and steel, cuts through the 135-year-old former arsenal's structural order. An 82-foot-high viewing platform (the highest point of the wedge is 98 feet) provides breathtaking views of modern Dresden while pointing towards the

exact area where the firebombing of Dresden began, creating a dramatic space for reflection.

The new façade's openness and transparency contrasts with the opacity and rigidity of the existing building. The latter represents the severity of the authoritarian past while the former reflects the openness of the democratic society in which it has been reimagined. The interplay between these perspectives forms the character of the new Military History Museum.

Its intention is to make a brash unprecedented statement that is almost unbelievable, though it is backed up with a meaning and rationale that is worth thinking about and discussing. The project demonstrates how architecture can embody a fashion and bring publicity value that can pay off when clients hire a "starchitect" to design a building in order to bring interest and fame to their organization. A new building can effectively create a buzz about the enterprise and its "brand"; the celebrated unveiling can generate a newsworthy moment offering a new and important cultural component to its surroundings. It can be exciting to keep abreast of what's happening in this world of cutting-edge design, and it promotes an ongoing interest in architecture.

These fashionable current projects generate commentary in the press and sometimes genuine controversy, which tends to pump up curiosity about the project. Sometimes the media critics will praise a building that the public finds unattractive or even dismaying, or sometimes the architect who is proud of his or her work may be surprised by its critical reception. Or a client and his or her architect may be thrilled with a project, only to find that the neighbors are upset. These strong emotions connected with buildings are a testament to how deeply they affect us. An awakening to architecture can be sparked by listening to these voices praising or damning a new building project.

It is curious that people can disagree so sharply about the value of a particular building. But as our interest and engagement are aroused, our confusion as to the role of architecture may increase. Is it only for the client who pays for the building? Is it purely a creative expression of an architect's vision? Must it contribute harmoniously to its neighbors and the texture of the neighborhood? A developing interest in architecture, and greater attention to it, leads gradually to a familiarity with one's own reactions, to careful attention to others' responses, to an increased understanding of some of the forces bearing on and helping to create the buildings around us, and eventually to a growing confidence in one's immediate reactions and opinions. Instead of feeling unequipped to understand the environment, one can become a more confident observer and critic of the surrounding environment.

AWAKENING TO THE REALITY OF ARCHITECTURE

Most of what we have been discussing in this chapter has been from the perspective of the person who experiences the environment—from the infant to the youth to the adult, gradually forming a relationship to the built environment. But our discussion above about fads and controversy highlights the fact that architecture isn't just created for us to appreciate. In contemporary society, architecture does not exist solely for the enjoyment and convenience of "we the public" that experiences these spaces and structures. It is initiated by the owners of the land who want to build for their own purposes. They may hope that the public will like the project, but often the building owners' main purpose is economic gain. The owners or developers are assisted in this endeavor by architects and builders who, in turn, have their own motives. Although they may intend to please the owner and the public, and certainly aim to make a living in the process, they may also likely seek to add strength to their own reputations as designers.

The goals and objectives of these factions—the public, the owner, the designer, and the builder—don't always harmonize; in fact, they may often directly oppose one another. The owner might put a premium on profitability, whereas the designer may overemphasize a personal artistic or formal exploration, with the partial aim of achieving greater fame and reputation. The public who experience and live with the project may have little sympathy with either of these motives, seeking only the pleasure of an accommodating and stimulating architecture.

When any of these individual goals dominates a project at the expense of the others, a certain amount of confusion and misfit may well occur. Excessive profit motivation can result in shoddy construction and cheapness of design. An overbearing design ego can produce a dramatic result that financially ruins the owner, whereas an over-zealous public can extract compromises that hurt the owner's pocketbook and drain vitality from the design. Successful projects require that all the actors eventually come together and commit to creating a harmonious result.

Assuming this cooperation produces a built project, how can we then evaluate the relative success of the result? Certainly, some built places are more significant architecturally than others. The next chapter begins to offer an exploration of the qualities that define "architecture." It attempts to cut through the confusion caused by architectural fads and controversies to uncover the core elements of good architecture. In it, we seek to develop a way of seeing the built environment that unites the multitude of places that inspire us and move us with their structural integrity, their deep utility, and their timeless beauty, illuminating our lives with the spark of delight. □

"A bicycle shed is a building; Lincoln Cathedral is a piece of architecture. Nearly everything that encloses space on a scale sufficient for a human being to move in is a building; the term *architecture* applies only to buildings designed with a view to aesthetic appeal."

—NICHOLAS PEVSNER, *AN OUTLINE OF EUROPEAN ARCHITECTURE*, 1943

"It takes more than putting building materials together to create architecture. No one can explain exactly what that more is, except that architecture has a spirit and building has not."

—FORREST WILSON, *STRUCTURE: THE ESSENCE OF ARCHITECTURE*, 1971

CHAPTER TWO

WHAT IS ARCHITECTURE?
(and What Isn't)

THE QUOTES ON THE FACING PAGE set the theme for this chapter: Is there really something that distinguishes a work of "architecture" from a mere "building"? If so, is it just aesthetic appeal? It turns out that the answer is a lot more complicated, and a lot more interesting.

Attempts to answer this question begin on the first day of a typical *Introduction to Architecture* class when we turn off the lights to show the silent mass of new students three images. The first shows a row of old stone houses with cone-shaped roofs along a road in southern Italy. The second is a 7-Eleven® convenience store in Los Angeles. The third image is of the medieval gothic church, Notre Dame, with its flying buttresses and gargoyle-studded parapets. Then we ask the question: "Are these all examples of architecture?" And this is what we get: A hand goes up, "Just the big church"; another hand appears, "Any building is architecture!"; a third: "None of these! They are all old and boring. What about that new mile-high building, the one that rotates, you know that shiny one in that desert town?" Then one of the few adults in the class slowly raises a hand, "What about my house? I've worked on it for years. For me that is architecture." We feel torn because we agree with all these answers, but there's just so much missing from them. Each answer is partially true and yet woefully inadequate.

Let's start with the first answer. Nothing surpasses a gothic cathedral as a prime example of the true essence of architecture. But this is not the year 1213, the world has changed, and we cannot make buildings like this anymore. As for the second response, it's easy to feel sympathetic to this one. Most of us remember when we were young, how hard we worked to make a play space from scraps of wood, and what a challenging and profound experience it was. Something important had been created. A place for plotting and planning. But as we grow up we usually realize that there's more to making a great place than merely making something to enclose a space. To the third answer, we must confess we too are often dazzled by the magic of the latest technology, the heroic and the dramatic, and the huge buildings that succeed in catching our attention. But these buildings have little to do with our everyday life, we'll likely never make one, we'll only occasionally visit one, all we can do is drool over the glossy magazine spreads. But the times we've actually visited one, it usually turns out to be fun for about five minutes, then it's exhausting because it doesn't feel as though it really relates to us. And to the last response, we want to assure this mature student that we've spent our entire careers assisting others to do just what she's describing. This has been our approach to work over the years, as it is for most other architects. It's creating and improving places for people to live, work, and gather, and to do it in a way that produces significant architecture.

So how do we respond to these answers on this first day of class? We first point out that making an important and significant building is similar to making any other worthy object; that is, it must be durable, useful, and aesthetically pleasing. Creating architecture is a bit like building a garden, a car, or a bridge. The difference between a wonderful creation and an offhand one—between architecture and an unremarkable building—is the special attention to these three aspects, and the care and feeling that go into making something that we are committed to. Where such a commitment is missing there can be a tendency to do just enough, to take care of the problem at hand as quickly as possible and call it a day.

A structure that is well built and long lasting, functionally effective, and stimulating to our perceptions, emotions, and thoughts in a pleasurable way can transcend mere "building" to become a work of "architecture." All three characteristics are required—the absence of any one prevents the building from being a true example of architecture. In architecture, these three virtues work together as naturally as they do in a good boat: well built to be safe and durable, and shaped to fulfill the vessel's specific function, which results in a form so simple and natural that we take great pleasure in observing and using it.

When a building exemplifies these three qualities especially strongly and clearly we may be able to learn something from it. The architecture can teach us how it is organized and integrated into a unified whole experience, if we know how to "read" it. What the poet Dryden understood about great poetry applies equally to architecture:

Would you in this great art acquire renown?
Authors, observe the rules I here lay down.
In prudent lessons everywhere abound;
With pleasant join the useful and the sound;
A sober reader a vain tale will slight;
He seeks as well instruction as delight.[1]

A recent house in Napa, California, by the firm Turnbull Griffin & Haesloop is a good example of how these "prudent lessons" can be

[1] From *The Poetical Works of John Dryden*, edited by Geo. R. Noyes, Houghton Mifflin, 1909, p. 916.

translated into architecture. The entry hall (drawing at left) functions as a connecting link to the main sections of the house while also showing the structural strategy in such a clear and powerful way that it makes a memorable and positive impression.[2] As a result, passing through this entry is a pleasurable experience.

But before we proceed too far down this path of the interaction of the three essential qualities of architecture, it's important that we first delve into the many ways the word "architecture" is used in our language. This exploration of the many uses of the term reveals the meanings it can hold for us in our everyday lives.

THE MANY MEANINGS OF "ARCHITECTURE"

We know from experience that the word can have different connotations depending on how we use it. For example, we sometimes think of architecture as referring to the characteristics of an *entire region* and its culture. Thus, we might say "the architecture of New Mexico," recognizing the patterns of form that have grown out of the cultural history and local materials of that region. In this case, these patterns might include the many indigenous forms created by the different Native American groups, the Spanish influences, as well as the modern structures that may or may not incorporate those traditional patterns.

---

[2] The entry doors on the right lead into a generous hall with a display table. A turn to the right leads down a few steps into the living room, whereas a turn to the left heads into the private bedrooms. Straight ahead matching doors lead out to a patio. This hall displays all the wood framing with its exquisite craftsmanship and structural order.

Looking east on San Francisco Street, Santa Fe, New Mexico

A variation of this might be the phrase "the architecture of Islam," which refers to a type of architecture associated with Islamic *culture and its history*, a set of building forms that often reappear in various locations in the world.

Then there are the expressions "medieval architecture," "Renaissance architecture," or "modern architecture," all referring to the buildings of a particular *style or time period*. It is through these regional, chronological, and ideological lenses that architectural history is normally organized and taught.

An image of Islamic architecture with its pointed arches, minarets, arcades, and interlocking surface decoration, the Imam Mosque, Isfahan, Iran.

59

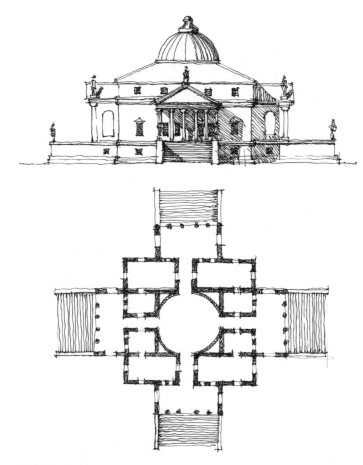

Palladio's Villa Capra.[3]

When referring to the work of an *individual architect*, we might speak of the "architecture of Palladio" or the "architecture of Frank Lloyd Wright," a categorization that is based on the architect's ideas, talents, and resulting designs.

---

[3] Palladio designed this country house, Villa Capra, outside Vicenza, Italy, in 1565 for a retired priest. This sketch is based on Palladio's drawing. The building, often known as Villa Rotonda, is probably the most influential house ever, having been an inspiration for 500 years of building in England, the United States, and throughout Europe.

One can also refer to "high-rise architecture" or "residential architecture," referring to the building *type* itself. And though the word is historically used to identify the act of designing and creating buildings, as in "the practice of architecture," it has also gained popularity in the digital age to describe the structure and organization of systems.

Frank Lloyd Wright's Fallingwater.[4]

But at the heart of each of these ways of using the word is the sense that we are dealing with structures that have been designed to satisfy certain functional criteria, to be durable and safe, and, hopefully, to bring aesthetic pleasure to the owners, inhabitants, and passersby.

These various examples of the use of the term *architecture* show that we need to clarify what we mean when we speak of architecture. Are we referring to the profession that creates it, to the "significant" buildings of history, or to the contemporary works currently in the news? Can we include the unselfconscious buildings of traditional cultures? What about the bulk of buildings in our cities, not all designed by architects, not all particularly distinguished or even interesting? And what about our own place, our home or apartment, the space that we live in every day, that we furnish, rearrange, and try to make comfortable and attractive? Is that place an example of architecture?

---

[4] Wright's Fallingwater in Bear Run, Pennsylvania, was designed for the Kaufman family in 1935–1936. It is arguably one of the 20 best examples of American architecture, and one of Wright's best works.

INFORMATION ARCHITECTURE

A discussion of the term "architecture" would not be complete in the 21st century without noting that it has been appropriated by the digital world of information technology, where the term refers to the structure of the computer software that organizes information. A good informational design is robust and stable, arranged to be easily usable. Hopefully, it will then be a pleasure to use.

Another use of the term, "virtual architecture," can refer both to "paper architecture," comprising structures that have been conceived, designed by an architect, but remain unbuilt, as well as the increasingly realistic digital 3-D worlds that many young adventurers have come to inhabit, explore, and navigate for countless hours each day through video gaming. And there are also popular games like Sim-City® that allow a player to create a whole new town, complete with an economy and a planning code.

Needless to say, this book will remain grounded in the realm of the physical, the tangible world for the most part, where the term "architecture" refers to what we might call "place-based form." Yet although these forms we inhabit are created to satisfy human needs, both physical needs and requirements on the one hand and emotional/intellectual and spiritual needs on the other, it seems important to acknowledge that the digital realm of information architecture increasingly exists as a kind of parallel perceptual universe to the physical world we inhabit, related to this world of physical form in part because it consciously draws on the design process of creating physical buildings of "brick and mortar" that exist in actual space/time.

For the purpose of this chapter, "architecture" will refer to any building that demonstrates a regard for firmness, utility, and aesthetic stimulation, regardless of how or by whom it was designed. This could include a barn erected by the local carpenter, a museum, an interesting house along the street, or a dignified downtown bank. Of course, we all recognize that only a few buildings so successfully integrate firmness, utility, and beauty that they are accepted as great architecture (Notre Dame Cathedral in Paris, Grand Central Station in New York, and the Disney Symphony Hall in Los Angeles, to name some obvious examples). But more modest buildings that also successfully knit together the three qualities must be included, such as the indigenous Trulli stone houses in Apulia, Italy, or the custom-designed wood homes of Bernard Maybeck in California.

Like most human enterprises, greatness occurs rarely, goodness occasionally, and well-intentioned efforts often. A great piece of architecture will perfectly integrate its structure and function, and do it in a way that moves us with its beauty and thoughtfulness. There are only a few truly great examples of architecture, but fortunately there are many that aspire to be good examples and succeed. Once we develop and hone an ability to discern the essential qualities that make architecture vivid and alive to us, the fact that our environment contains many thoughtless and unpleasant buildings will not prevent us from taking pleasure in those examples of architecture around us that at least partially succeed in integrating structural, functional, and aesthetic needs.

LOOKING AT INDIGENOUS ARCHITECTURE

A broad view of architecture includes not only big, expensive public buildings and projects but also any well-built, well-designed, and interesting "background" buildings, including modest, private, residential structures that comprise much of the built environment around us. In 1964 Bernard Rudofsky published his *Architecture Without Architects*, with photos of indigenous buildings from around the world, structures that weren't designed by architects and that weren't self-consciously trying to be art, but that possess the same organic beauty that we associate with nature.[5] Indigenous architecture is characterized by the use of local, readily available materials and adherence to local building customs, while still allowing for individual expression and adjustment to unique personal needs. Examples are shown in the two images below: on the left, the breeze-catchers on houses in Sindh, Pakistan,[6] and on the right, a bazaar from the same area (from a 1905 postcard).[7] Rudofsky argued that these indigenous structures indeed exemplify significant architecture because they are so skillfully built, directly fit the needs of the users, and yield such beautiful results.

[5] Bernard Rudofsky, *Architecture Without Architects: A Short Introduction to Non-Pedigreed Architecture*, New York, Museum of Modern Art, 1964.

[6] "These ventilation towers are topped with a wind catcher, oriented to provide cooling breezes in summer and to function as light catchers during the winter." From Rudofsky, op. cit.

[7] Shikarpour Bazaar, in Hyderabad-Sindh.

North African Bedouin tent of woven goat hair.

Humankind created buildings first out of a basic need for protection, shelter, and survival. Often these immediate shelters were spontaneous and rough (think of a log cabin, igloo, or prairie sod house). Though very simple, they possess a dignity and genuineness that comes from their being hand-made from immediately available materials, and maintained through constant repair and embellishment. Tents and tepees, often made of woven animal hair or animal skins, are appropriate for cultures moving with their herds or game. Their lightness and simplicity makes them mobile, easily packed up and moved to new locations where prospects for food and water may be improved.

In some settled communities an unfortunately high percentage of people do not have access to resources that allow their structures to advance beyond a level of emergency survival shelter. The intention to create architecture, as we have defined it, is not very relevant for those struggling merely to survive—this situation requires immediate, makeshift shelter in order to satisfy purely functional requirements. Periodically, an earthquake or flood may temporarily thrust a community back into survival mode. At these times, architecture as an expression of the three values becomes irrelevant. It is important for us to realize that the notion of architecture can only start to grow out of a state of relative safety, satiety, and peace. Architecture, like art, can begin to emerge only when survival is assured—when more refined needs and desires can be addressed and confidence in the future encourages more investment in permanent structures.

We can experience this emergence from immediate shelter to a fitting, comfortable sense of a "home" by noticing our own behavior on a three-day camping trip. When we first arrive we select a spot to pitch a tent, start a fire, and fix our dinner. After surviving our first night, we make improvements, adjusting the tent position to a more level spot, removing rocks under our sleeping bag, and building a stone windscreen for the fire. If it rains and blows on night two, we add a rain screen to the entry of our tent, drive our tent poles in more firmly, and pull the fire area closer. We find that we are gradually improving our dwelling condition, making our tent more stable and stiff, and rearranging the elements to make them more functional and convenient. This natural instinct to improve our surroundings, to make them more enduring and useful, is one of the essential first steps toward architecture.

Indigenous architecture develops among a group of people over many generations and centuries, but it starts the same, with individuals responding to their immediate environments, each attempting to improve their own situation. As good solutions are hit upon, neighbors adopt them. Gradually, over time, effective strategies emerge and become accepted cultural patterns of building.

Through the warp of these accepted patterns of building, each individual builder weaves his own weft of personal needs, preferences, and skills, creating an individual building that shares its underlying DNA with the surrounding community of buildings. This combination of community-patterned order and individual variation is akin to natural growth patterns of living organisms that follow a system of genetic rules in a responsive and adaptive manner. Most of us recognize the great beauty that emerges in the natural world, and we see that same kind of beauty in the buildings of traditional indigenous cultures. Like organic growth, indigenous architecture is governed by agreed-upon patterns of form. In addition, each individual builder and craftsperson brings an inner aesthetic sensibility to the work, adjusting and embellishing it to produce an individualized,

unique, and personally satisfying result, similar to the others but with its own special flavor.

Rudofsky was right to bring attention to indigenous building and to call it "architecture without architects." The best of indigenous building can be considered "architecture." It is a product of a hand-built technology (which requires repair and maintenance to survive) that directly, honestly, and even boldly addresses a functional need, and that is beautiful because it is both ordered and varied, patterned, yet unique—just like nature. It is one extreme on a scale that places unselfconscious building at one end and highly intellectual, self-conscious, and studied building at the other; from design by anonymous users to design by professional architects and engineers. Some surviving examples of indigenous buildings are especially significant examples of architecture due to the constant repair and adjustment that they have received in order to last over time. This aspect of renewal leads not only to their survival but also to an ongoing improvement in their functional fit to the site and to the occupants' needs. We can sense this "fitness" in spite of our not being of that culture, the appropriateness to its time and place of any object—building, basket, tool, or rug—that has developed its form over many years in response to the minds and hands of its users.

Women reapplying mud plaster to an adobe building in New Mexico.

Another strength of indigenous architecture stems from this periodic renewal—as with the yearly whitewashing of indigenous Greek houses or the re-mudding of African earthen structures—giving the buildings a freshness and liveliness. It is evident that the buildings are really used, which makes them feel "alive," playing active roles in their inhabitants' lives.

ARCHITECTURE MADE BY US ALL

If indigenous cultures can create architecture through the individual efforts of nonarchitects, why can't we do the same with our own, similarly unprofessional efforts to make gradual improvements to our individual spaces and homes as we adjust and improve them over time, just as we did on our three-day camping trip?

In our own rooms, we move the furniture and activity spaces around trying to find the best spot for reading, sleeping, and dressing. If we own our house, we may reinforce the structure against earthquake, or improve the ability of the building to endure by replacing the roofing material, cleaning gutters, or doing termite repair work.

We improve the usefulness of the house by adding a deck, shading a patio, or planting a deciduous shade tree. And we improve the aesthetics of the place over time by repainting, bringing in a rug, tearing down an unwanted wall, and so on. These are all essential architectural activities, adding to the strength, usefulness, and beauty of the building.

Moving beyond our own home, to what extent do the neighboring houses, shops, banks, and civic buildings in our town embody the concept of architecture? If we put ourselves in the shoes of the designers of these buildings, we will recognize that they were, for the most part, trying to make these buildings strong, useful, and to some degree attractive. Any building that has been erected in the last 75 years has been reviewed for structural adequacy by the local building department to ensure that it meets a minimum degree of safety. And buildings are so expensive to construct that they are inevitably designed with a certain amount of utility in mind given that they must provide a return on the owners' investment. These two factors tend to be more deeply embedded in buildings than aesthetics—not because the designers didn't want them to be attractive, but because the "art" of the building is more likely to be considered a luxury, perhaps something that can be added later. This is in sharp contrast to the natural emergence of beauty from the structure and its use that we most often find in indigenous architecture.

But if you look more closely, you might start to notice the evidence of an architectural aspiration on the part of some designers, either laymen or professionals. There may be high-quality materials employed that will lengthen the life of the building, or effective incorporation of intelligent features that shelter the entry, block out unwanted summer sun, or permit needed winter light. Careful site planning may permit greater use of the outdoor spaces or a better relationship to the street. And other features might be executed in such a way as to bring special attention to the building, to give it more visual impact, or to increase the sense of importance of the building or to communicate its function. Each of these elements can contribute to the architectural value of the place.

This is not to deny that it is easy to spot buildings that have taken serious shortcuts, at the expense of quality, usually to save money. Examples abound: Mini-marts and strip malls are especially prone to this single-minded design for maximum rents at a minimum price. A building can look cheap because it is, scrimping on solidity and durability and giving no thought to beauty.

Our society's earnest but nonprofessional efforts to create architecture today have had limited success, unfortunately. One likely reason is the increasingly transient nature of our culture. We often don't live in the same building or neighborhood long enough to really understand how it might be improved. Another reason is that we tend to see the buildings around us as commodities, things to be bought and sold, used until they are worn out. And we are often seduced by images of what is fashionable and trendy, which when built lead sometimes to a dated look as soon as a new fad becomes popular.

But these shortcomings should not blind us to those successful aspects and elements of the buildings around us when they do occur. Almost every building has some features that can be accepted as emerging from the architectural instinct to unify firmness, utility, and beauty—a few will have none, and a few will have many. When a building is maintained and improved over the years it can attain a measure of real value. This durability and usefulness automatically radiate a kind of beauty, a sense of "rightness."

INDIGENOUS ARCHITECTURE VERSUS ICONS OF ARCHITECTURE

A gulf exists, of course, between the great bulk of utilitarian and unpretentious architecture created by the lay community and the more heroic and powerful architecture that is created for symbolic reasons and is deemed to be "more important." The great iconic buildings are what we think first of when we talk about architecture: pyramids, temples, cathedrals, sports palaces, and commercial centers. But we must try to bridge this gulf if we are to see the common spirit of architecture that unites these two extremes.

A typical Greek village sitting at the base of a high promontory consists of many individual homes and shops, each created out of culturally accepted material, technology, and shape as well as community agreements about width of streets and relationships to neighboring buildings. Although each individual effort possesses admirable aesthetic qualities, a second level of significant architecture emerges from the resulting village—a unified, harmonious place with infinite variety, a whole environment. The symbolic, more important structure, such as a temple to the gods, is built on the heights above the town, designed by individually talented artists employing precious materials, exquisite craftsmanship, sophisticated geometry, and great expense and effort.

The village shown at right offers real architectural experience: a substantial building fabric that is intended to permanently establish a sense of place, sensible structures that respond to the daily life and needs of the community, and wonderful sensual

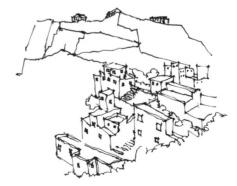

The remains of the Parthenon, Athens, Greece.

pleasures that stem from the scale of the spaces, the textures of the materials, and the thermal pleasures of cool interiors during summer. The village offers an ongoing hubbub of additions, repairs, and maintenance that permits growth and gradual change.

Now if we compare the architecture of the village with the temple on the hill—the Parthenon in Athens, for example—we will note many differences: Instead of a collaborative form emerging from the acts of many separate but cooperating individual builders, the Parthenon, like most other Greek temples, stands alone as the work of single designers. Whereas indigenous village architecture's order consists of agreed-upon patterns that each builder varies slightly to fit his particular situation, the order of the Greek temple is based on mathematical proportions and exact dimensions. In the case of the Parthenon, the visitor supplies the variety by moving through and around it; and whereas indigenous architecture can usually retain its original qualities even after being partially demolished and added on to, the Parthenon is fixed: Built as a single polished jewel of eternal form, it cannot be added on to and lives now as a ruin that we reconstruct in our imagination.[8]

---

[8] The Parthenon, finished in 432 B.C.E., was actually designed by two architects, Iktinos and Kallikrates. A very accurate copy of the building in its original condition can be visited in Nashville, Tennessee.

In spite of the important differences between indigenous architecture and the monuments that we typically study in history, they share even more important similarities: They both must effectively deal with the forces of gravity and weather through the intelligent use of materials durable enough to last; they both emerge from a direct human need for the space, for shelter, commerce, or worship; and the finished form of both types of architecture offers a kind of beauty, pleasure, or awe to the user.

This same architectural contrast is equally evident in a 12th-century French village, except that the Gothic cathedral is located in the middle of the town rather than atop an adjacent hill. Again, the town's individual buildings comply with local conventions of material, design, and interaction with neighboring structures. Yet each structure expresses the specific needs and desires of the users, as well as decoration around the entrances that may state the purpose and hopes for the building. These individual "ordinary" buildings have real aesthetic value: We can take pleasure in the solid elemental materials of stone, wood, and plaster, and in the ever-varying streetscapes of homes, shops, and pedestrian traffic. The whole town-form itself is really one large piece of architecture.

The Gothic churches of 12th-century France—each built by local labor and craftsmen but directed by a single architect—amaze us today with their magnificence.
Their clear and direct floor plans lead the worshipers into the church, down the aisles, toward the transept, to a pew for a sermon or an apse for communion, or to a side niche for private prayer—but always under soaring vaults of upper structure supported by thin pillars with huge

The Gothic cathedral is an iconic image of architecture.

windows in between, flooding the interior with light. We are simultaneously aware of the seemingly delicate stone structure of the building that has stood for nine centuries so far, the perfect fit of the church to its purpose of building a faith through the lessons of the sculptures, the sermons, and the choir, and the extraordinary sensual and intellectual beauty and harmony of all its physical, visual, and acoustic aspects.

FIRMITAS, UTILITAS, VENUSTAS

We have been describing architecture in terms of three vital qualities: firmness, utility, and beauty—the elements first enunciated by Vitruvius in his *Ten Books of Architecture* during the 1st century B.C.E. Vitruvius asserted that all the various types of buildings:

> Must be built with due reference to durability, convenience, and beauty. Durability will be assured when foundations are carried down to the solid ground and materials wisely and liberally selected; convenience, when the arrangement of the apartments is faultless and presents no hindrance to use, and when each class of building is assigned to its suitable and appropriate exposure; and beauty, when the appearance of the work is pleasing and in good taste, and when its members are in due proportion according to correct principles of symmetry.[9]

[9] From the translation by Morris Hicky Morgan, Harvard University Press, 1914, Chap. III. A later translation by I. D. Rowland and T. N. Howe, Cambridge University Press, 1999, translates the triad as "soundness, utility, and attractiveness."

Vitruvius of course wrote in Latin, and his durability was *firmitas;* convenience was *utilitas*; and beauty was *venustas*. In English, we are most familiar with the translated words of Sir Henry Wotton: firmness, commodity, and delight. To these, we can add more synonyms:

No matter which set of terms we use, these three qualities remain indispensable to the way we understand what distinguishes architecture from mere building.

FIRMITAS	UTILITAS	VENUSTAS
stability	convenience	beauty
firmness	commodity	delight
strength	functionality	economy and completeness
resilience	usefulness	interest
durability	workability	order and variety
redundancy	serviceability	good proportion
sustainability	adaptability	coherence, unity
in balance with earth	in balance with man	in balance with itself

As reflected in the last item in each category above, this trilogy has been more recently emphasized in a slightly different way by Stanley Abercrombie in the conclusion to his book *Architecture as Art*, where he states:

> The three relationships at the heart of architecture are that of a building to the earth, of a building to man, and of a building to itself.[10]

This broadens and enriches Vitruvius's triad, helping us to capture more of the essence of architecture. The building must come to terms with the *earth:* not only the earth's gravity, but also its weather, seismic

---

[10] *Architecture as Art*, Van Nostrand Reinhold, 1984.

activity, and seasons must all be handled comfortably by a work of architecture. This includes graceful weathering (which may involve the capacity to be modified and repaired over the years). And because the materials of construction come from the earth, the relationship includes the energy, effort, and any associated damage to the environment resulting from their extraction, as well as the preciousness and rarity of the materials. Finally, the earth offers a site for the project, which the building comfortably settles into or awkwardly stands out from.

Architecture responds to *man*, to those who conceive, build, and eventually use it. It accommodates man's size, physique, and gait. Its size and proportions fit us and our gatherings with others. We measure the building's dimensions by comparing them to ourselves, and the arrangement of the building responds effectively to our intended use for it. The building fits within our budget. The building fits into our community's accepted rules of appropriate land use and building design (zoning restrictions).

Architecture's relationship to *itself* implies a unity and wholeness to the building. In this sense it is a unique entity, made up of integrated and cooperative parts, similar to the harmony between all the parts of our whole body. For a building to have a satisfactory relationship to itself it must transcend its *firmitas* and *utilitas* (the needs of the earth and of its owners and users) and embody a personality that people in the society can react to, can have an aesthetic, sensual, or intellectual response to. The building will have an integrity of its own, a coherent appearance, message, and mood.

ARCHITECTURE OUT OF BALANCE

It is sometimes difficult to sort out the concept of "good architecture" because at different periods of history the triadic equation becomes unbalanced, with one or another aspect being overemphasized at the expense of the others. This is especially true in architectural education, where the emphasis shifts from age to age, and decade to decade, as the faculty attempts to correct previous architectural excesses or shortcomings.

This very question—What is architecture?—would not have come up at the École des Beaux Arts design school in Paris during most of the 19th century. The École was the most influential school of art and architecture in the Western world, emphasizing the Classical style and attracting students from all over the world. At the time, the school's form of instruction was regarded as the most appropriate method of architectural design and training. But starting in the 1870s, the approach it taught began to be challenged by a succession of new ideas about what architecture should be and how it should be made.

The Beaux Arts paradigm was supplanted by Modernism in the 1920s after World War I, which was then challenged by Postmodernism in the 1960s, and replaced in turn by a scattershot of theories emphasizing either psychology, post-structuralist theory, culture, semiotics, biological form, or computer-generated form, for examples. Not only have the theories of what architecture is about been changing rapidly, but so have society's needs: from affordable postwar housing to the structure of mega-cities, from new technological and scientific laboratories to a commitment to sustainability and conservation. And since the late 20th century new tools available to architects, mainly computer-aided design and the use of the computer in manufacturing, have transformed the day-to-day methods of architectural practice, and more important, transformed the character of the buildings produced via these tools.

The Beaux Arts education attempted to raise the general level of professional architectural practice through a rigorous and competitive program of design exercises combined with apprenticeship in the design studios of the upperclassmen. The emphasis was on composition of the building, selection of the best style for the particular problem, and a beautiful drawing and rendering of the proposal. If the design problem (also called a "program") happened to consist of a new government complex, the student's first task was to select the most appropriate style (gothic or Renaissance?), followed usually by a symmetrical site plan of building elements and a highly perfected drawing of the plan, section, and elevation, along with typical details of decoration appropriate to the selected style. Students learned historical precedent, composition, and extraordinary drawing skill. But there was little if any attention paid to the uniqueness of the site or client, to the particular aspects of the building that would make it function more efficiently or effectively. Nor was cost a consideration. It was a magnificent education in certain areas, but it tended to overemphasize aesthetic aspects at the expense of firmness and utility.

But as programs became more complex—like the design of a train station, for example—the Beaux Arts skills were manipulated to manage the new functional needs. One still got a "historically correct" style and composition as seen from the outside, but it included subdivided interior spaces to provide for all of the required modern functions. The American architect John Russell Pope finished his many years of architectural training at the Beaux Arts school in Paris and returned to the United States for his distinguished career in commercial, institutional, and residential work. His 1919 Union Station in Richmond, Virginia, has a classical form that is reminiscent of the ancient Roman Pantheon, a temple to Roman gods, but it is in fact a rather complex train station, where each space serves for waiting, ticketing, baggage, lunch, or restrooms.[11]

Modern architecture began in the early 20th century partly as a rejection of the idea that one could design a new building by picking a historical style. Instead, the design would emerge from the necessities of the building's intended use and the economics of its construction. Any beauty in the resulting design would emerge from the elimination of the superfluous, and from adherence to the users' objective and specific needs. Le Corbusier, the French/Swiss modernist, was an admirer of rationality; thus he tried to solve problems by dissecting their

[11] The building has survived and now serves as a science museum.

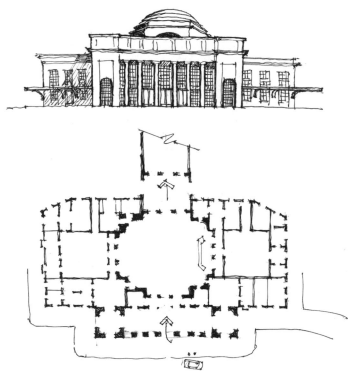

Union Station, Richmond, Virginia.

elements and separating the conflicts between them. His plans for a
Radiant City consisted of high-rise residential structures widely separated by acres of green space and auto highways separated vertically
from the pedestrians below. Unfortunately, this concept ignored the
inhabitants' needs for close contact with nature, neighbors, and nearby
shopping facilities; where the concept has been tried, it has resulted in
sterile acres of identical isolated domiciles perched high up in the air.
"Corbu," as he came to be called, flew to give a lecture in America in
1935, and in the same year wrote a paean to the airplane, glorifying its
absolute functionalism and technical daring.[12] Applying this same

---

[12] Le Corbusier, *Aircraft*, London, The Studio Ltd., 1935.

Palace of Assembly, Chandigarh, designed by the Swiss/French architect Le Corbusier in 1955.

approach to buildings, his ideal image and vision for architecture at the time is captured by his famous statement, "The airplane is a machine for flying. The house is a machine for living."

In spite of his rather abrupt and narrow statements, and his extensive use of the modern industrial material of steel-reinforced concrete, his other architecture is often wonderful, in part because he was also a painter and most often imbued his buildings with expressive gesture, proportion, variety, texture, and color.

The Modernist credo of functionalism does, in fact, contain a powerful and lasting insight into what makes good forms. Drawing partly from the unself-conscious indigenous creation of beautiful buildings and implements, and partly on the magnificent results of newly developed rational technologies, Modernism promised a new, clean, pure beauty that would emerge from a direct incorporation of functionalism and structural expression, trusting that any resulting aesthetic worth would emerge naturally, without any conscious attempt to create "art." [13]

---

[13] The Modernists would subscribe to the "beautiful tool" analogy—the belief that any object that is purely functional, and purely technically efficient and sound, will automatically be beautiful.

This pure and idealistic vision in the work of Modernism's greatest architects, such as, Walter Gropius, Corbusier, and Mies van der Rohe, resulted in magnificent, bold, and exciting buildings. But this exalted vision was not able to support the following generations of modern architects. Due perhaps to commercialism and to a rigid and narrow application of modernist theory, the successive work did not often live up to its earlier standards, and modern architecture started to feel simply brutal, harsh, cold, and even inhuman. Older homes were torn down and replaced by more economical apartments, and aging neighborhoods were occasionally replaced with "rational" higher-density high-rise housing blocks. These modernist replacements seemed to drain the environment of its color, variety, and sense of place. A particularly egregious example of this unsuccessful urban renewal was the Pruitt-Igoe development in St. Louis, designed to replace a depressed neighborhood with affordable housing in 1954. The project (partly influenced by Le Corbusier's Radiant City image of separated towers) proved to be such an inhuman environment that, starting in 1972, it was torn down by the city. By the 1960s a revolt against modernism

The Pruitt-Igoe mass housing project in St. Louis, Missouri, by Leinweber, Yamasaki & Hellmuth. The entire project was eventually pulled down by the city.

was under way, both among the public and within the schools of architecture.

During this same period, the University of California at Berkeley created a new College of Environmental Design (covering architecture, city planning, landscape architecture, and graphic design) under the direction of William Wurster, and it embarked on a new building to house the college in the late 1950s. The resulting Modernist design,[14] was in the Brutalist mode, all raw concrete, perhaps influenced by Gropius's Bauhaus building at Dessau, Germany, and by another important and recently built architectural school of the time by Paul Rudolph at Yale, and by Louis Kahn's Salk Center at La Jolla. But the building, finished in 1964, now housed a new crop of students (and some teachers) who were disenchanted with the recent round of buildings that modernism was spawning. In reaction against it, architectural teaching, particularly on the West Coast, took a turn toward the humanistic, the social, and the psychological. Attention was now focused on the psychological experience of the users in buildings: Did buildings promote healthy social interactions, were they open to all segments of society, did they encourage individualistic, free behavior, or did they regulate uniform standards?

And so the 1960s hippies confronted the crew-cut 1950s. In this West Coast version of architectural education at the time, firmness and aesthetics were de-emphasized in favor of a broadened notion of usefulness, appropriateness to culture, and satisfaction of basic human psychological needs. The center of attention shifted to utility, but a special form of utility, namely the usefulness of the environment as an enabler of self-actualization, freedom, and psychological health. The important question became, "Is the environment healthy for the individual and the community?" During this period, good architecture was now viewed as sharing more of the characteristics of indigenous

---

[14] The design team consisted of Joe Esherick, Vernon DeMars, and Don Olsen, all members of the architectural faculty.

models, where owner-builders worked with the land, built structures by hand with the aid of the community, and used more informal available materials. But this period was unlike indigenous architecture in that there was no community-accepted form for the buildings, so that each owner-builder was

An alternative, owner-built, back to the land, anti-modernist dwelling.

free to follow his or her inner muse. The result, of course, could be wildly inventive and chaotic, but always warm and homelike.

Another related revolt against modernism took place at the same time, one that rejected pure functionalism in favor of a re-acceptance of history and precedence, often accompanied with wit and clever messages referring to the clients, the site, or the architect. Postmodernism, as it was termed, employed exaggerated references and proportions, as exemplified by Michael Graves's Portland Building of 1985. The symmetrical facade plays with classical allusions, such as the implied giant keystone (which has no structural function) and a 35-foot-tall sculpture of Portlandia, a quasi-mascot for the city, holding a trident in one hand and reaching down with the other to welcome visitors to the building.

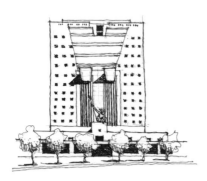

Postmodernism in the 1970s was followed by yet another revolt against modernism, which occurred mainly on the East Coast of the United States and in Europe. It was later given the name Deconstructivism, and like

The Portland Building was probably the first and most influential Postmodern building. Among architects, its users, and city residents, the design remains controversial.

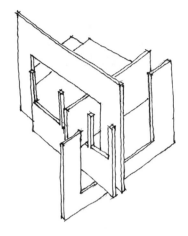

Postmodernism it played with the disruption of traditional forms and approaches to structure and function. In Deconstructivism, all three Vitruvian goals—firmness, utility, and what was nominally thought of as delight—are intentionally de-emphasized in favor of theoretical thinking and the formal rules of composition that generate the forms. Any delight that such a design generates is as much intellectual as sensual. An abstract set of geometric rules (some drawn from the history of the site and some borrowed from literature or philosophy) would be adopted and then manipulated, like the linguistic rules of a language, to create a design. The sketch above, after an analytical diagram of Peter Eisenman's early House VI (the Frank residence of 1972–1975), illustrates the intersecting planes and volumes that he played with to eventually generate the design of the house.

If a "column" didn't reach the floor (but hung, in fact, from above, as in House VI and in his later Wexner Center of 1983–1989), the intention was for us to reconsider our normal expectation and understanding of a column, to re-evaluate our automatic thinking, and so to expand it. It is in fact "anti-structuralism," a purposeful upsetting— not only of our expectations but also of the actual structure that supports the building. And if a column happens to land smack in the path of a stairway, it can be considered as purposeful "anti-functionalism," again shaking up our assumptions of what is appropriate, causing us to re-evaluate what is reasonable.

This intentional upsetting of structural, functional, and even aesthetic common sense can obviously lead to discomfort and even anxiety among some inhabitants of the building. Eisenman was clearly interested in making the inhabitants uneasy: He saw this as one of his roles as an architect. In his famous 1982 debate with Christopher Alexander concerning the proper role of architecture in modern society, he declared:

> I am not preaching disharmony. I am suggesting that disharmony might be part of the cosmology that we exist in . . . . I do not believe that the way to go, as you suggest, is to put up structures to make people feel comfortable, to preclude that anxiety.

Eisenman believed that architecture, like sculptural art, is the manipulation of materials according to abstract rules and ideological strategies. Where his buildings incorporate hanging beams that don't rest upon posts, or posts that don't actually reach the floor, the intention is in part to challenge our ordinary structural intuitions and understandings, creating confusion and surprise. He takes the same approach toward function: His House VI includes a continuous skylight, window, and floor light that forces the owners to sleep in separate single beds on each side of this feature. Eisenman called this approach "post-functionalism," which often resulted in spaces that frustrate normal functions. What remains are the challenging aesthetics, which are really quite fascinating in their mix of order and disorder.

Eisenman, as architect, pushes the envelope by treating the essential triad of firmness, utility, and delight as foundations against which to push and react. The structural realities are masked (sometimes mocked) and antistructural puzzles are introduced; some of the functional necessities such as a convenient and comfortable

The atrium stair of the Wexner Center for the Arts, Ohio State University, with its hanging column.

room layout are replaced with puzzlement, frustration, even anxiety. What remains is a novel and exciting sculpture to inhabit, one that thwarts expectations; a work of art that also contains an obligatory kitchen and bath. And for the Frank family that commissioned it, it is also "architecture." They received the building/sculpture they had hoped for, one that they could live in and enjoy for its unconventional qualities.

WHAT ISN'T ARCHITECTURE (BUT COULD BECOME SOMEDAY)

From the previous section, we see that the Vitruvian triad is always to a varying degree involved in architecture, even when one aspect is emphasized over the others, or when an aspect is opposed and challenged. A work of architecture can de-emphasize or even intentionally contradict one or more of Vitruvius's triad—firmness, utility, and delight—and still clearly be architecture. But the triad can never be ignored—each aspect is addressed in a work of architecture, hopefully in ways that express clear points of view. Structures that avoid any one of the triad aren't architecture. This is the key.

There are so many buildings in the environment that cannot be considered architecture as we are defining it. For example, conventional storage facilities are intended to store materials safely and se-

curely, but that is all. Because no one is intended to occupy the units longer than the time it takes to deposit or withdraw belongings, there is no attempt to make them attractive, comfortable, or interesting. Architecture is for people to use *and* enjoy; when structures are made for the purpose of simply warehousing belongings, they are not intended to be architecture. But this is not to say that a storage facility or almost any structure for that matter cannot be subsequently transformed into architecture, though this feat may require an especially inventive imagination.

Another example along the same lines are buildings that are pre-designed and manufactured to be structurally sound and to serve a specific function, but that are not intended for living in and contain no plumbing or electrical utilities or other internal amenities. These buildings are not architecture—rather they are structures that can be bought off the shelf, set into the environment, and later developed to function as the owner sees fit.

What is interesting about these buildings is that, depending on how you look at them, the structures themselves have architectural possibility. By using these structures as a "shell" one can conceivably create architecture. This can be done by creatively adapting them to active human needs and uses. A premanufactured building can start to take on architectural value, for example, when the wide open column-free structure is placed on a perfectly smooth and level concrete floor and fitted with adequate distributed lighting so that it can be used as a vast, uncluttered workshop permitting unobstructed work on large objects.

In fact, a recent trend is to use a series of premanufactured or recycled units as modular building blocks to assemble a variety of building types like shops, kiosks, residences, and even churches, resulting in structures that are not only stable and strong, but functional and delightful as well. Adam Kalkin, one of many architects who are currently working with prefabricated elements, recently combined

Large, open, clean shops invite us in, to create, repair, be creative, and have fun.

a prebuilt Butler structure with shipping containers to create the house at left.

An early example of this approach of putting a building together using preformed industrial components was most eloquently developed by Ray and Charles Eames in their own Los Angeles home in 1949 (drawings below). The building was #8 in a series of Case Study Houses. The house and grounds are now designated a National Historic Landmark, and can be visited by appointment.

As we consider structures made from premanufactured elements, we need to remember that these elements can be utilized to create architecture, but that they are not necessarily architecture in themselves.

What about prototypical "stamped-out" designs, identical buildings that are placed on different sites without modification? Is a big-box outlet, a chain burger joint, or an individual gas station an example of architecture?

These buildings were originally designed by someone probably trying to make a firm, useful, and, if not beautiful, at least memorable building. But then the design was repeated over and over again in city after city, with only minor modification, and most often without responding to the site or to the surrounding buildings. In this important sense, such an endlessly repeated example cannot be considered architecture.

On the other hand, we should remember that some of the forms that are so ubiquitous and unremarkable to us today were once very creative and novel. A good example is Richard Neutra's 1947 design for a gas station that was innovative for its time (drawing below). That was architecture: A fresh, original design serving a new practical need.

And what about developer housing, where four or five individual designs are conceived and then duplicated hundreds or thousands of times throughout a development? The original plans can occasionally be considered as architecture due to their structural soundness, intelligent functional design, and basic attractiveness. But they necessarily suffer from one important handicap: They have been designed to be inoffensive and generally acceptable, without any delightful (or bothersome) eccentricities that would make them one of a kind, unique. The buildings haven't been shaped for a particular family, nor have they been designed around the particulars of the site and orientation to the sun. This brings a certain deadness to the designs.

Norwalk Gas Service Station, Richard Neutra, 1947.

Adding a front porch with a trellis, a distinctive roof over the entry, and a little landscaping are good examples of architectural features that enrich a building, adding value, function, and aesthetics.

Yet we cannot dismiss those aspects of the tract housing units that are admirable: Their uniform construction and design bring economies of scale to bear so that they are more affordable. They often offer sensible zoning between public and private spaces, and they usually offer generous front and back yards. But what is most hopeful about these housing developments is that they have the potential to be continually modified, remodeled, and added to over the years by each family.[15] This might begin with landscaping in the front yards, where each owner adds personal touches to the front of the house, with the intention of creating a more pleasant street view and providing a more gracious entry into the house. After several years, a second story may be added. Over many years, the units can take on a striking individuality in spite of their original uniformity.

What isn't architecture now can start to become architecture tomorrow through fresh thinking and gradual transformation via repair

---

[15] An exception is condominiums and neighborhood associations where individual modifications are not allowed. Individual adaptation and variety are sacrificed in favor of uniformity, order, and a consistent group form.

and remodel. Architecture begins when people address a real human need and embark on a design process that gradually does the following:

- shapes the building in response to the physical demands of the site and climate, ensuring that the structure will protect the inhabitants and endure, preserving the client's investment
- shapes the building in response to the needs and desires of the inhabitants, making it work and function smoothly
- shapes the building to bring pleasure and delight to the senses and to the intellect

Architecture doesn't consist of only the biggest, most expensive, most well-known projects. Architecture doesn't have to be large in scale, expensive, public, or noteworthy. It can be modest, gently fitting in, well-behaved, and silent until needed, like a British butler. To create architecture, each of us can work to improve the spaces we may have influence over by continually modifying those aspects that are less appropriate and replacing them with elements that help to cure and repair. Many of us can use this instinct of architecture to improve our small corner of the world. Some of us may be inspired to commit ourselves to a life's work of helping others achieve their architectural goals. All of us can try to help keep the flame of architectural passion alive in our own lives by being attuned to our environment, rewarding those examples of successful environments with use and praise, and recognizing that less successful places have the potential to be gradually transformed with care, knowledge, and investment.

In the next chapters we will look in more detail at each of the above three aspects of architecture that, when engaged together as a whole, differentiate it from mere building. We hope that you will then be able to use them yourself to analyze how well the built spaces you come across are actually achieving their architectural goals. And we hope that this approach will help enrich your own experience of place. □

"Most laymen seldom look at architectural structures, or ask the simple question, 'What makes buildings stand up?' This apparent lack of interest in structures is due to a misapprehension: that an understanding of structure requires a scientific mind and the acquisition of technical knowledge usually outside the province of ordinary citizens. This fear is unjustified."

"In addition to speaking to us about usefulness, economics, energy, and safety, structure asks us to appreciate creativity and beauty. It is no wonder that some of the greatest minds of the past have given themselves to the study and the creation of structure, and that all of us, more or less consciously, are interested in discovering the mysteries of its laws."

—MARIO SALVADORI,
WHY BUILDINGS STAND UP: THE STRENGTH OF ARCHITECTURE, 1980

CHAPTER THREE

FIRMITAS:
The Strength of Architecture

THE ROMAN TEMPLE MAISON CARRÉE in Nimes, France, was built of stone and completed in 20 B.C.E. It is still in great shape. After the collapse of the Roman Empire, its use changed from temple to church. Since then it has served a dizzying array of alternate uses, from private residence to stables to town hall and public archive. Since 1823 Maison Carrée has been home to a museum. After 2,000 years and counting, it is still a working, beautiful building, having withstood constant use, variable climate, earth movements, and alterations.

In stark contrast, modern construction tends to have quite a short lifespan. In Great Britain the average lifespan of a new building has shrunk to 132 years, whereas in the United States a building is expected to last on average only around 74 years. And in China, which as we all know is experiencing a booming and rapidly expanding economy, the average lifespan of a building is a mere 30 years. China's problem is not only the huge flow of money and ambition but also fast-track design and construction and "economical" engineering. The very short lifespan causes a big drain on

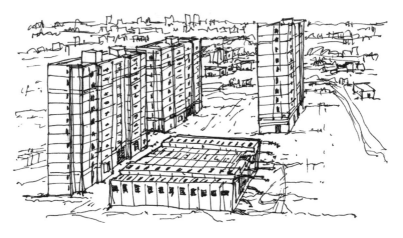

Shanghai apartment building collapse, 2009.

the environment, mostly because large amounts of material and energy needed for construction must be replaced so often. And this rapid pace can also lead to very serious structural failures. One of the most spectacular failures occurred in June 2009 when a newly constructed multistory residential building in Shanghai toppled over as a single unit. Fortunately, the building wasn't yet occupied, but one worker was killed in the incident. The collapse occurred when dirt excavated from one side of the building for a new parking garage was piled onto the opposite side of the building, creating uneven soil pressures across the building's footprint. Rain then softened and added weight to these soils, which eventually caused the whole building to slide toward the excavated hole, off its hollow (and unreinforced) footings, and finally tip over onto the ground.

Structural failures are, of course, not the only or even the primary cause of the shortening lifespan of buildings worldwide. The major factor in the limited longevity of these buildings is simply that they are not constructed in a way that ensures long-term use through ongoing reparability and adaptability. The main reason for this is that it can be more costly to build durably. Another reason that perfectly usable buildings are torn down and replaced is simply to accommodate changing fashions.

But whether or not a building is able to stand the test of time, the making of a building for human use must always begin with the creation of a safe structure as an absolute imperative. This is why Vitruvius places *firmitas*—or firmness—first in the triad of necessary qualities; it is the primary precondition for both safety and longevity. He views *firmitas* as consisting of strength, stability, and endurance and explains how the design of a sound Roman edifice begins with the suitability of the underlying soils followed by the depth and width of the foundations. Vitruvius then goes on to describe the proper thickness, shape, and size of the walls, which in turn depend on the selection of appropriate structural materials. He ends with notes on the careful detailing of the structure to prevent damage and decay through the destructive actions of water, wind, and heat. This list of precautions developed over two millennia ago still guides our approach to structural design today.

Of the three essential characteristics of architecture set forth by Vitruvius, only the absence of *firmitas* is dangerous. When a building falls short in meeting functional requirements or is not aesthetically pleasing, it is a sadly missed opportunity. But if a building were to collapse on us, the result could be tragic. Throughout the centuries, rules of thumb and builders' experience provided structural adequacy for modest buildings. And this is still partly true. If a builder replicates the structure of a similar building, using the same kinds of structural members for the same general uses with similar sizes and spacing, then the structure will likely be adequate. But there is also the danger that an important structural function of a particular element can be overlooked. Although laymen sometimes jump right in and remove a wall here and add a picture window there, professional builders, designers, and architects tend to be more cautious, first determining whether these wall sections are crucial for stiffening the building or holding up loads from above. These professionals have the training and experience with structural issues to assess how the structure works as a whole and to take on responsibility for the building's structural safety.

Vitruvius's treatise continues to be a relevant guide to many of these issues facing architectural practice, even though the underlying reasons for ensuring firmness and strength were taken for granted in his time. He didn't specifically mention the safety of the builders during construction, or of the later inhabitants using the building. Culturally, this requirement had already been understood many centuries earlier by Hammurabi in 1700 B.C.E.: "If a builder builds a house for someone, and does not construct it properly, and the house which he built falls in and kills its owner, then the builder shall be put to death." A serious responsibility indeed!

Firmitas first and foremost ensures the occupants' safety during extreme situations like earthquakes and storms, but a structure that fully incorporates *firmitas* offers many other significant qualities as well. Let's look again at the other aspects of *firmitas* that we offered in the last chapter:

- stability
- firmness
- strength
- resilience
- durability
- redundancy
- sustainability
- in balance with the earth

Firmness, strength, and resilience together create stability, which is key for the safety of the inhabitants when buildings undergo the extreme pressures of high winds, snow loads, or earthquakes. These qualities are also important if there are changes to the underlying support of the ground due to water or landslides. Durability refers to the structure's longevity, its ability to withstand the many years of weather and other forces that impact the materials of construction and all the joints between the materials. The structure must also withstand years of human use: people trudging over the floors, making minor changes to the walls, and inadvertently banging and kicking all the surfaces. Redundancy is the structural overcapacity that preserves firmness and strength even if some part of this capacity is removed. This could occur either by the overconfident removal of a wall by a homeowner, or by a falling tree landing smack in the middle of an occupied living room. (A tree actually did fall through the roof of one of our projects, and thanks to redundancy in the main roof beam that had been designed a bit larger than necessary, no one was hurt.)

Sustainability, the next item on our list of *firmitas* qualities, also implies that the structure is durable and can thus be maintained, repaired, and even modified in order to extend its life over many years, preventing the need for demolition and the use of new materials to create a totally new facility. In those cases where replacement is absolutely necessary, a carefully demolished building can be partially salvaged and thus reborn into a new structure. A building that is environmentally sensitive is also constructed so that its spaces contribute to the thermal comfort of the inhabitants. Thick adobe, stone, or concrete walls accomplish this by tempering the extremes of outside temperature, storing heat and coolness in their thermal mass instead of allowing the rapid thermal transfer of heat or cold through a wall (as can occur with a thin glass facade), which can require excessive mechanical air-conditioning to maintain the users' comfort.

Finally, staying in balance with the earth means that the materials used in the structure are plentiful, renewable locally sourced, and healthy. Although we may be able to maintain fir forests sustainably through careful management and replanting, we must take care not to ruin the less renewable supplies of precious woods. Other materials that require major quantities of energy in their fabrication, like steel and aluminum, must be used with restraint and economy. Plastics that not only require precious amounts of fossil fuels in their manufacture but also are not recyclable and give off noxious fumes in a fire must also be used with great caution, if at all.

These are the facets of *firmitas* that we need to take into account now and in the future. Each one contributes to the important aspects of longevity that allow a building to adapt to changing uses over time, to be repairable after damage, and to age gracefully. This inclusive *firmitas* also ensures that a structure appears and feels firm to the inhabitants, is ecologically sound, and is a good investment of materials and energy. In general, a building may be useful and even aesthetically pleasing, but if it isn't built sustainably and can't take the punches of weather, use, and modification, it will likely not last for many years and it simply can't be considered a good example of architecture.

We will conclude this chapter by exploring how structure can have a role in our aesthetic appreciation of the building: how structure itself has the potential to be deemed beautiful, and how it can also become provocative and challenging. Let's look at each of these aspects in more detail, starting with the most fundamental: the ways stability, along with other considerations, provides a safe refuge for a building's inhabitants.

ENSURING PHYSICAL SAFETY

There are many ways we might endure relatively minor injuries as part of our daily use of buildings or any environment we may find ourselves in: The danger of a slip, a fall, or a bump on the head is, unfortunately, ever present. But the intention behind *firmitas* is essentially to guard against the drastic effects of a building collapsing on us, burning us, or choking us with smoke or fumes.[1] Humans have learned, through

---

[1] In the chapter on *utilitas* we will discuss how the design of the building can prevent inhabitants falling, being trapped, or getting trampled and can ensure that people with varying physical capabilities can effectively access and use the building.

trial and painful error, how to build more safely. A heavy, stoutly built structure may save us from invaders and protect us from bad weather, but the same structure might harm us if it were to fall down during an earthquake or a tornado. Light structures, like tents and delicate wooden buildings, won't crush us under a sudden avalanche of tons of stone and concrete, but they may blow over in a powerful gust of wind; a well-engineered light wood-framed building will sag, perhaps tilt, but if it fails, it will fail slowly, not suddenly.[2]

Some noteworthy historical examples that illustrate the process of how builders learned to build safely include the Hagia Sophia in Istanbul and the Beauvais cathedral in northern France. Hagia Sophia was constructed between 532 and 537 C.E., but a couple of earthquakes brought down the eastern arch of the dome only 21 years later. Rebuilt, the dome lasted until 989 C.E., when the western arch collapsed. Subsequent repairs lasted until 1346, when the eastern arch fell again due to earthquake. Finally, in 1847, an iron chain was installed around the base of the dome to resist the pressure of outward thrust. Similar learning on the job occurred when the main vaults of the choir at Beauvais cathedral in northern France collapsed in 1284 and the later tower collapsed in 1573 (never to be rebuilt).

These structural failures didn't cause the huge loss of life that residential areas have suffered during earthquakes, which have been the main foe of heavy masonry residential structures over the years. The fourteen most deadly quakes between 525 C.E. (Antioch, Turkey) and 2004 (Sumatra) each took a staggering toll of between 80,000 and 140,000 lives. These fatalities were almost all caused by falling unreinforced (or poorly reinforced) masonry buildings. Even in recent history, structurally deficient buildings have killed inhabitants during earthquakes and windstorms. The latest 2010 quake in Haiti tragically exceeded all of these, resulting in over 200,000 deaths, again mostly caused by falling buildings.

---

[2] See Ralph Gareth Gray, "Riding Out the Big One," *Fine Homebuilding*, January 1, 1991, pp. 60-65.

Although light wood-frame buildings have a much greater ability to survive earthquakes because of their lighter weight and greater flexibility, they are especially vulnerable to wind damage from tornadoes. The 2011 tornado in Joplin, Missouri, simply blew down wood-frame buildings (and trees and vehicles) in its path, scattering the pieces to the winds and resulting in over 130 fatalities. Another problem with wooden structures is that they are vulnerable to burning down unless adequately fireproofed, and even today aren't generally well protected. Here in the Bay Area we particularly remember the 1991 Oakland–Berkeley fire in which almost 4,000 homes burned to the ground and 25 lives were lost. That we learn so reluctantly is highlighted by the fact that virtually this same area was devastated by fire 70 years earlier in 1923, with 640 homes lost.

We can't prevent earthquakes, tsunamis or other flooding, tornadoes, or forest fires, but we can design buildings that help the inhabitants to survive them. Earthquakes can occasionally be so powerful that we cannot expect even our strongest buildings to emerge unscathed. In the case of small buildings with few inhabitants, it is usually too expensive to guarantee that they will be unaffected by such a seismic event. Instead, as architects, engineers, and owners we compromise and accept some level of cosmetic damage and minor structural deformation, while still ensuring that the overall configuration of the building is maintained and that it doesn't collapse on the inhabitants. Very large and expensive buildings are designed to withstand the biggest foreseeable quakes, but they will rock and roll and swing from side to side during such an event. Inhabitants will feel these large movements, and may be injured by moving objects inside the building, but will almost certainly survive.

In the Midwestern United States, tornadoes are common, and small wooden buildings can't withstand the strongest of them. The traditional defense has been the inclusion of a cellar where people retreat and wait out the storm. Beyond sturdy shutters, little can be done to prevent damage to large expanses of window and sliding glass doors. Steep roofs with big overhangs and broad, thin walls act as sails in a strong wind. To survive, a wood building would do better to be low to the ground, lack roof overhangs, have smaller shuttered window and door openings, contain a number of stiffening walls, and be very strongly bolted down to a heavy foundation. Because such a design isn't often opted for, an alternate approach is to build out of heavier materials—such as masonry, stone, or even multiple layers of plywood—rather than framing with thin wood studs. The weight of the resulting building alone will make it safer during a tornado.[3]

Floods are most easily avoided by building higher than the flood plain. But especially severe flooding that rose well above the normal flood plain in the central United States in 2011 resulted in extraordinary damage to the homes and businesses that lay in these lowlands.

Some fatalities can and do occur during floods, but it is the vulnerability of a wooden structure to fire that can be the real killer. Wood buildings can be perfect matchboxes, given that they are constructed of many relatively small sticks of wood, arranged closely together, that can blaze up quickly in a raging bonfire. You might think that fires in small wooden buildings wouldn't be so fatal because it would be so easy to simply run out of them. But a fire can often smolder undetected for several hours, only erupting into a serious fire after the inhabitants have gone to sleep, usually in a different room, further postponing awareness of the danger. The carbon monoxide gases emitted by a fire can also be fatal. People also often run back into the burning portion of a building to rescue family members, losing their lives in the process.

There are several steps we can take to mitigate the danger of fire in a small wooden building, many of which are required by the building

---

[3] "I went to Miami two days after Hurricane Andrew to do a story on what buildings made it through the storm, and which ones didn't. I learned that houses with steep gables, designed to attract 'snowbirds' from New England, were sitting ducks. Low-pitched hip roofs stood the best chance. Incredibly, very few houses had storm shutters. They could have kept the flying roof tiles out of a lot of houses. And once the tile breaks the shell of the house, it's over. Attached trellises and deck roofs were like the clasp on a zipper—pull here to open." From Chuck Miller, former West Coast editor of *Fine Homebuilding*.

code: arranging multiple exit paths so that if one is blocked another is available and including extra fireproof gypsum (drywall) wall and ceiling sheathing, both inside and out. Other ways to prevent a deadly fire are to use large wood structural members that don't burst into full flame so readily, and to provide heat and smoke detectors to give earlier warning, as well as a fire sprinkler system that is turned on by temperature automatically. Finally, cabinets, carpets, and other interior finish materials and furnishings are increasingly available that are either fireproof or eliminate the emission of toxic fumes when ignited.

Larger steel-framed buildings are not generally flammable in themselves but can become dangerously infirm if the steel isn't protected against the heat of a fire. Steel starts to yield and deform at 1,400°F, so it must be insulated against such high temperatures either by a sprayed-on insulation, sheets of gypsum, or a coat of concrete (turning it into reinforced concrete). Escape from a large building that is on fire is assisted by the design of accessible exit paths that lead directly to the street and that are protected from the rest of the building by fire doors. An important job of the designer and builder, then, is to ensure that a building is firm and durable enough to protect its inhabitants' lives during catastrophic quakes, floods, wind, and fire.

Another potentially dangerous load on the structure is the weight inhabitants themselves place on it, both by their collective bodies and by heavy objects that are stored in the building. Floors need to be strong enough to support not just the typical loads of the users but also the weight of a whole party of guests, sometimes just standing, but sometimes dancing in rhythm to the beat. If this dancing (or marching or wind gusts, in the case of a bridge) rhythm corresponds to the natural harmonic vibration of the underlying structure, the deflections can build upon one another, like the waves in the ocean, getting larger and larger until the structure collapses.

In spite of all our efforts to make buildings structurally safe, occasional tragic events do occur, claiming lives and causing injuries. Architects, like doctors and civil engineers, have a sacred responsibility

Tacoma Narrows Bridge in Washington State shortly after collapse due to rhythmic deflections caused by wind, November 1940.[4]

to avoid unnecessary risk to users' lives and limbs. But architecture deals with such a broad range of issues that specialization is usually necessary. The nature of the work of designing a building has become increasingly complex over time as the types of construction, materials, and technologies have evolved and multiplied. Because of these changes, the architect or designer can no longer possess all of the detailed expertise that is required to ensure that the building is strong, durable, and safe. Today, specialists in structural engineering, code compliance, and even waterproofing are invariably part of the design team.

We have talked about how the baseline of safety needs to be guaranteed by a stable, firm building. But what is really meant by stability and firmness? Does it mean rigidity? What enables a structure to develop a resistance to the forces on it? We will see that a building's shape, weight, and connection to the ground all have a role in its stability. How its main structural elements—arches, posts, beams, and connections—are arranged is critical to its stability. And the various materials of construction must also be stable. Stability is the fundamental goal of structural design.

---

[4] Check out the 1940 newsreel covering the collapse on YouTube™. Fortunately, no human lives were lost.

UNDERSTANDING STRUCTURE

Even though we now rely on the expertise of structural engineers and other specialists to take care of a complete building design, there is no reason the layperson can't have a basic understanding of and appreciation for how structures work.

The basic qualities of stability, strength, and resilience are in evidence in forms all around us, even in our own bodies. Beginning students of architecture sometimes confess their fear of not understanding the mathematics and physics that underlie the science of structural engineering, worrying that this will hinder their eventual success in the field. It is true that a degree in architecture requires a couple of courses in structural engineering, which aren't always easy for some students.[5] Although these courses do introduce some important mathematical formulas along with the basic structural principles, the most helpful ones tend to emphasize an intuitive and qualitative understanding of structural ideas and analysis.

When all these levels of stability are achieved, the building will maintain its structural usefulness over many years of predictable climatic stress, shifting ground, and the impact of heavy use. The building will perform well, responding to the changing forces applied to it over the years. We will see that a firm, stable building is in reality not totally rigid. Instead, it is always moving in small but measurable and recoverable ways in response to the forces on it, similar to the motion of a mature tree.

[5] A wonderful introduction to the role of structural engineering in architecture is Mario Salvadori, *Why Buildings Stand Up: The Strength of Architecture*, W. W. Norton, 1980.

ENSURING THE STABILITY OF THE WHOLE BUILDING

In order for a building to provide a safe haven it must successfully maintain its position and orientation under the influence of many different kinds of external loads: the earth's settlement and expansion under it, the earth's shaking during an earthquake, and the powerful gusts of a strong windstorm coming from unpredictable directions. The term *load* means the forces or pressures that act on a structure. These forces are measurable: They can be assigned a quantity. Some forces act in a vertical direction—like gravity—and some horizontally—like wind. Horizontal loads are called lateral loads.

Let's take wind first. As wind strikes the side of a structure it pushes on the building sideways. For the building to maintain its position it must push back against the wind force with an equal and opposite reaction, using the stiffness in its structure and the friction between it and the ground upon which it sits.

If the building had no internal stiffness to maintain its shape in the face of the wind, it would simply collapse onto the ground like a house of cards. If the building was internally stiff but sitting on wheels (or on a slick frozen lake), the wind would start to move the building away from the oncoming wind. The only force that resists this

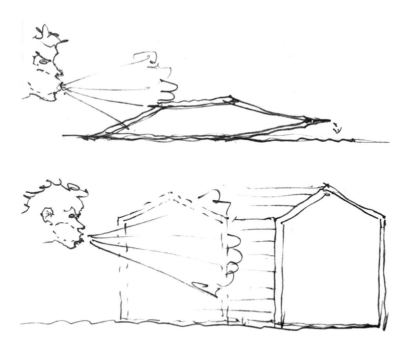

horizontal movement is the sideways friction at the base of the building, between it and the ground it sits upon.[6]

Now assuming the building is stiff enough to maintain its shape and has enough friction with the ground so that it doesn't slide away, there is a remaining challenge that the building must meet: It must not rotate or tip over. In a wind force from the side, for example, the building's weight and broad stance will help to stabilize it. A lower building, hugging the ground rather than standing up tall, will also help (see the sidebar on the facing page).

These reactions to wind can easily be modeled and therefore visualized by blowing horizontally on a paper box and observing it either collapsing (because it wasn't stiff enough to maintain its shape) or

---

[6] The fishing ice-houses in Minnesota don't, in fact, get blown around by the wind because the ice is covered with snow, creating enough friction and resistance to keep them in place.

PIVOTS, PRESSURES, & MOMENTS

As illustrated in the drawing below, the wind is pushing on the entire upwind facade of the building, exerting a pressure of so many pounds per square foot, and can be considered as equivalent to a single large wind force, F_w, pushing against the building somewhere near the midpoint of the building's height.

Whereas friction at the base prevents the building from sliding sideways, the wind force tries to rotate the building away from the wind, pivoting around the fixed foundation on the lee side of the wind. The building resists being rotated clockwise through its sheer weight, F_B, which can be considered as a single force acting straight down near the center of the building.

The wind is trying to rotate the building clockwise around the pivot point (P), and the weight of the building is resisting by trying to rotate it counterclockwise around the same point. Like a lever arm, the wider the building (W), the longer lever arm the building's weight has to counteract the wind: Similarly, the taller the building (H), the longer lever arm the wind force has.

The ability of a force to either rotate an object or to resist that rotation is called moment, and it is defined as the amount of force multiplied by the length of the lever arm at which it acts. In the case of the building here, it is resisting the wind's effort to tip it over with a moment of its weight times its lever arm, or $F_B \times W/2$. The wind's overturning moment is its total force acting at a point halfway up the building, or $F_w \times H/2$. Who will win? For the building to be stable, the resisting moment of the building's weight times half its width must win.

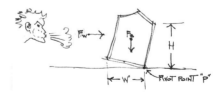

sliding along the smooth floor away from the "wind." Increasing the friction between the box and floor (putting the box on a rug) will prevent the sliding away. But another instability will then be observed, namely that the windward side of the box will start to rise, with the box rotating away from the direction of the blowing. This rotation can be prevented by adding some weight to the top of the box.

For the building as a whole to be stable, then, it must do three things: maintain its shape, resist translation (moving along in a single direction), and not rotate around any point of the structure.

THE "FEEL" OF STABILITY

A firm and durable building handles all the forces (loads) acting upon it comfortably, which means that it doesn't move (much) or rotate, and isn't bent out of shape by them. Furthermore, it can withstand a lot more force—shifting ground below, increasing loads on the floors above, or an unusual weather storm—before actually succumbing and failing. A firm building will also resist destruction by a wrecking ball or other impacting object, but only up to a point. The firm building has excess capacity (or redundancy), more ability to withstand these forces than will likely be required. But the building does move a bit as it develops the necessary resisting forces, and when the applied forces are relaxed, the building hopefully returns to its original condition.

We can empathize with the structure of a building by paying attention to how our bodies react to similar forces acting on it—we can pretend to be a building. In order to stand upon our feet successfully, our body needs to resist (i.e., hold up) not only our weight but also the added packages we might be carrying. Our bodies can comfortably handle quite a bit of additional weight—up to a point—beyond which we are likely to collapse. As we begin to reach that point, we can feel the increasing pressure (stress) throughout our body, up through our spine, legs, and feet. We can even feel an accompanying slight shortening of our whole frame as we absorb the increasing weight.

On the other hand, hanging by our hands from a bar reverses these internal forces, and we feel not the compressive stress pressing down on our body but rather a tensile or pulling stress, all the way from our grasping hands, along the length of our arms, through elbows and shoulders, down our spine, across our pelvis, and down through the legs. Our bodies will actually lengthen a bit during this hanging. Under compressive force, we not only get a little shorter but also a little wider, and under tension we not only get longer but also a little thinner.

Because of our body's natural resiliency, when we put the load down, or when we stop hanging by our hands, we expect our bodies to return to their original length. After exercise, we don't expect to have permanent deformations in our body.

Similarly we don't want permanent deformation in our buildings after they have been subjected to a load. This ability to spring back to the original dimensions after the release of loads is termed *elasticity*.

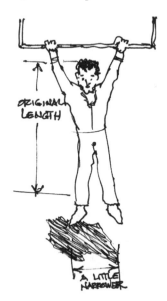

We can also understand lateral or sideways forces on a building by paying attention to how we deal with standing in a strong breeze or maintaining our balance on a bus or subway. In these situations we resist being tipped over by widening our stance, giving ourselves a broader base, just as a building with a wider base can better resist the

overturning moment created by the wind. We can also better maintain our equilibrium by leaning over into the wind, letting our body be held up by the force of the wind. This also reduces the force of the wind by presenting a slightly smaller area to it. But the wind could cause us to slide sideways if we were standing on an icy sidewalk with little friction between it and our shoes.

To build a human pyramid, we start with the biggest and heaviest folks at the bottom and end with the smallest and lightest at the top, in order to get a bigger wider base, to lower the center of gravity of the group, and to reduce the toppling rotation of overturning created by any wind blowing on the group. Buildings traditionally have benefited from the same strategies of a wider base, a lower center of gravity, and reduced wind loads.

To stiffen our bodies to maintain a position or posture we triangulate our limbs, creating a stable rigid triangular

shape, either by widening our
stance or by supporting our head
with a crooked arm.

Another vivid illustration
of the stability of triangulation is its use in countering the outward
thrust of roof beams. If you lean heavily over a table to support your
weight, it will be very helpful to hold on to a tensioned string or rope
with both hands, as this tie prevents your arms from slipping out to
the sides, causing you to collapse onto the table.

Most of the physical forces that act on and within buildings can
be analogously felt in our bod-
ies. This sympathy with how
a building will perform helps
us to design them more intel-
ligently, and to better understand why they sometimes fail.

STABILITY OF MATERIALS:
STALKS, STONES, SKINS, AND MUD

How have humans throughout history used materials to build firm
structures that are stable, long lasting, and in harmony with the earth?
Until structural engineers achieved the capacity to calculate with a
computer how, in detail, a structure responds to earthquakes and
wind, designers based their design on examples already built, modifying them until they got into structural trouble, indicated by cracking
or unusual displacement. At that point they either patched up the
structure or simply retreated to an earlier successful scheme. Experience was the teacher, and experiment the technique.[7]

---

[7] The Romans reached the amazing 42.4 meter span of the unreinforced concrete dome of the Pantheon in 128 C.E.,
and this span was virtually unchanged by Brunelleschi's Duomo (45.5 meters) in 1436 and St. Peter's dome
(42.3 meters) in 1626. Bigger spans were made possible only by steel framing or reinforced concrete.

Humans have always used the materials from the earth that we could get our hands on, sometimes refining them, then assembling them in combinations and configurations that have been more or less sturdy and safe. To understand the different qualities and characteristics of these various materials, it is helpful to put them into four broad categories: Stalks are linear elements that can take tension with some amount of bending and compression. These range from reeds and tree branches to hewn beams and posts, to metal bars, beams, and columns. Stones are heavy and hard, can take compressive forces but less tension, and include native rocks as well as quarried stone. Skins are thin sheets that can take tension within their surface (like a tight drum head) but do not resist much force perpendicular to that surface. They first came from animal hides, then woven cloth, followed by thin panels of wood, plastic, or glass. And mud, a wet soil mixture that can be poured and molded into forms, can take some compression when dried but very little tension. Mud was combined with stalks of reed or chopped straw to form adobe bricks, fired to form clay tile, and, finally, refined to form concrete, now typically reinforced with steel rods.

Regardless of the elements of construction and the strategies for combining them into building shapes, we are always limited by the inner abilities of the materials themselves to resist the loads that will be applied on them during the life of the building. Each material has a specific strength, a capacity to resist compression, tension, or both. And each of these has its limit beyond which the material will fail by breaking into pieces or by deforming to such a degree that it can no longer function structurally.

A more detailed look at how different materials respond under loads is beyond the scope of this book, but we can mention the fundamentals here. Each construction material—wood, stone, concrete, and steel—has a unique behavior when stressed. They all respond to compression by shortening and to tension by lengthening—just as our bodies do—but each by a unique amount. Stiff materials like concrete and steel don't change length by much; flexible materials like wood change length much more. And within a limited amount of stress—again, unique to each material—they all have the ability to return to their original length after the load is removed, like a rubber band or your body. This is their elastic behavior.

But one of two things can happen if this modest stress is exceeded. First, the material may accept the higher stress but will not return to its original length after the load is removed. Steel, and to a lesser extent wood, act like this. These materials will be permanently deformed, and the building that is composed of them will thus also be deformed. Not good, but not necessarily tragic.

The second possibility is that the material will simply and suddenly break apart under the larger stress. This is how stone and unreinforced concrete act: They can't take much tension before splitting apart, and although they can take considerable compression they suddenly crush and fragment under an excessive amount.[8]

A well-designed building keeps its materials of construction safely within their elastic limits, say around 60 percent of what they could safely carry if they had to. This is the margin of safety, the degree of overbuilding that owners have to pay for (and contractors may complain about) but which allows the designers to sleep well at night. It is one form of the redundancy of structure that allows the building to successfully withstand any unexpected stresses and modifications, adding to its long life and the lives of its inhabitants.

STABLE ARCHES AND DOMES

Stalks, in the form of flexible reeds, were first bundled together to form shelters by the Egyptians and others throughout the Near East. A current echo of this technique is the training of tree branches to

---

[8] Even steel will suddenly snap apart under its ultimate tensile capacity.

interconnect overhead, forming an arched canopy to shade an outdoor gazebo.

Later, the reeds were covered with mud to form a composite wattle-and-daub structure. The resulting vault-like structure can be imagined as a kind of precursor to reinforced concrete construction.[9] We can associate this interweaving of stalks with basket-making, where all the stalks share the bending forces along their length and with each other, resulting in a strong yet flexible structure.

In areas where long stalks of reed were not available, mud mixed with reinforcing straw and dried in the sun became bricks that could be stacked up into walls. Four thousand years ago in the Near East these sun-dried bricks were used not only to build walls but also vaults over the walls.

Adobe is still sometimes used in residences, but the great advances were the transformation of mud into fired bricks and into concrete via cement, and the

---

[9] America's Plains Indians, blessed with vast buffalo herds, covered their teepee poles with skins rather than mud, a prototype of a wood-framed residence of studs sheathed with plywood, or even a steel-framed high-rise sheathed with a skin of glass.

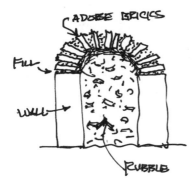

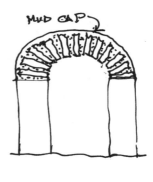

eventual replacement of straw with reinforcing steel. Now the "mud" can be poured into forms of any shape to create a reinforced concrete structure.

More durable structures were built where stone was available, chiseled into rectangular blocks for solid walls or into special shapes for arches and vaults.[10] But the Near Eastern vaults of adobe and the later concrete and cylindrical stone vaults of the Romans all share a structural challenge: The materials of construction can take lots of compression, but they will break apart under too much tension. It is possible to create an arch in which all the material is in pure compression by shaping it in the form of a catenary curve—the shape assumed by a necklace of beads when hung upside down. If this shape becomes stiff, it can be turned over to create an arch shaped in the form of an upside-down catenary. In this catenary arch, all the stones will be in pure compression, just as the hung necklace is in pure tension.

---

[10] We continue to use stone for building today, of course, but usually cut into thin panels for use as paving or the outer skin of a high-rise, or simply as interior veneers.

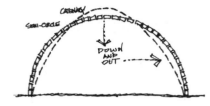

But since Euclid humans have preferred simpler geometric forms—circles, squares, and rectangles—even when they may not be the most efficient shapes structurally.[11] At left is a sketch of the problems that occur when the purely compressive catenary curve is rejected in favor of a half-circle. First, the arch is quite flat at the peak, making it tough to hold up in position, and the day the structure is completed the top portion will deflect downward a bit under the weight of its materials. Only friction between the rocks will prevent its collapse. Second, the middle portions at the sides already bulge outward from the line of pure compression (as shown in the drawing above), but as the peak continues to settle downward a bit, it pushes the sides even further out, putting their outer edges in tension. This causes the outer edges to break apart. Both of these actions can result in the vault collapsing.

The magnificent dome of the Pantheon, completed in Rome around the time of Vitruvius, solved these problems by leaving the top of the dome open to the sky (called an oculus) and then surrounding the hole with a thickened ring under compression. The half-circle shape on the interior is also strengthened by the addition of a massive amount of concrete on the outside, pushing the dome inward to counterbalance its outward thrust.

Other solutions to the problems of a circular arch are familiar to us: The top of the arch is fitted with a keystone, a specially shaped element with inclined edges

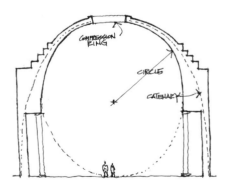

[11] Antonio Gaudi is a notable exception, basing his design of the Familia Sagrada Cathedral vaults on catenary curves.

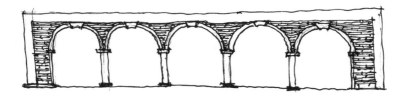

that can take both compression and vertical support from its neighbors. And the arch is partnered with more arches on each side, with filling stones in between the arches, so that the outward thrust of one is counteracted by the other. This goes on and on until a more substantial wall at the end can withstand the outward thrust of the last arch.

STABLE POSTS AND BEAMS

In forested areas, wood is either taken directly from the felled tree, hewn, or milled to form posts and beams; in industrial cultures, iron is mined, refined into steel, and fabricated into shaped columns and beams. Except in the case of stacked log building, beams span across upright posts, capable of resisting both compression and tension. The structural details that explain how beams support loads across an opening are somewhat complex, but a simple insight into how they work can be experienced by physically acting like a beam, by creating a plank with the body (as often occurs in a yoga class) and noting what it takes to keep our body rigid across the span between our hands and feet. How are we able to resist the tension on our stomach and the compression on our back? We and the beam do the same kind of work,

 deflecting downward a bit under load, putting our underside under tension and our top under compression.

Post and beam buildings are called trabeated structures in contrast to arches, and they have their own unique challenges: First, how to connect the posts and the beams together; second, how to stiffen the resulting building against wind and earthquake as we illustrated earlier. The Greek temples of stone were trabeated structures, with the stone beams (lintels) spanning very short distances to minimize tension and depending on gravity to keep them attached to the supporting columns. The temples had inner sanctuaries of stone walls that stiffened the structure, and thick, heavy columns that are hard to tip over.

Mortise-and-tenon joints connect the wooden posts and beams in medieval timber buildings (and in some high-end contemporary residences), and the framework is stiffened both by wooden diagonal braces and by the wattle-and-daub infill between the posts and beams. The weight of these buildings also stabilizes them against the wind, though not against an earthquake.

In contemporary wood-frame residential architecture the connections between the wall studs and the beams resist force from all directions, usually by way of metal plates attached to each member with nails or bolts. But the framework is relatively light and must be stiffened, usually by nailing on a plywood skin to the outside surface of the framework, and the whole structure needs to be firmly attached to a concrete foundation. In steel-frame construction, the joints connecting the various elements are either bolted or welded.

It is common to think of building structures as composed of floors, walls, and roofs, and most wood residential architecture is built of just these components, from the ground up. But cooperation between these elements is structurally advantageous and economical, and that is the role of the connections between them, the topic of our next section.

STABLE JOINTS, TRIANGLES, AND PANELS

For the most part buildings need to offer horizontal floor surfaces. Similarly, walls are most convenient when they are vertical, in line with gravity so they are balanced and to allow for furniture to be moved up against them and for the walls to become display and storage surfaces. These vertical walls and horizontal floors need to be connected to each other in ways that produce solidity and firmness in the whole building. But simply stacking floors on top of walls and posts doesn't produce the necessary lateral stability by itself—the whole assembly can be tipped over with a simple push. What is needed is to make some of the connections rigid, resisting any shift in the relationship between the elements they connect. Such a connection is called a moment joint.

Steel members can be welded at their connections such that the joint is as strong as the member itself. Less effective is to overlap the steel members and bolt them together. Wood elements can't be welded to each other, but they can be overlapped, glued, and screwed together to approximate a rigid connection. Reinforced concrete joints can be made rigid by interweaving the steel reinforcement bars from one element to the next before casting the surrounding concrete.

Moment joints in steel, wood, and reinforced concrete.

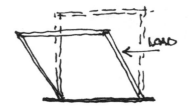 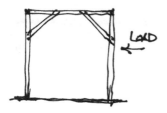

But let's step back a moment (pun intended), and remember how builders in the past made moment joints before the availability of steel and reinforced concrete technologies. They often used triangulation, linking the two main elements by adding a third member across the joint. This is called a brace. A brace creates a rigid moment joint because any movement of the trio of members would require that one or more would have to change in length. A nonbraced connection can simply tip over without asking any member to change its length. In effect, a triangular brace can create a (nearly) rigid moment joint.

Instead of just triangulating the joints of a structure, one can similarly triangulate an entire structural bay with a single long diagonal brace. The 15th-century building illustrated below shows a good

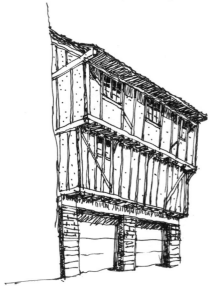

example of such braces on the second floor, but there is a compromised example on the third floor, where the diagonal brace is cut and interrupted by a window, reducing its value as a brace.

Triangulation as a way to strengthen frameworks can be seen in much of nature. A vivid example is the small structure inside the bones of a vulture's wing,

where the triangulation virtually forms a truss, allowing the wing bone to be very stiff but very lightweight.[12]

In the bone, the triangulation is not just in a two-dimensional plane, but rather forms a three-dimensional pattern, like a space frame,[13] giving the bone stiffness in all directions. Also note how the material is thickened at each joint between the frame and the triangular braces. Typically, more material is required at joints simply to accommodate and strengthen the attachment of piece to piece. The joints in our fingers, wrists, elbows, and so on all demonstrate this same thickening. This is true whether the joint is moveable—like our fingers—or nearly rigid, as in the inner structure of the bone shown above. The thickening of the joints in the bone structure above is virtually identical to the thickening in the forking of a tree's branches. In both cases the transition is smoothed by additional material— really triangulating material at the joint, like a solid brace—allowing external loads to more safely "turn the corner," flowing from larger to smaller branches instead of creating a crack at the fork.

STABLILIZING SHEAR PANELS

Thus far we have discussed materials as stone-like elements and linear elements (posts, beams, braces). But materials are also fabricated in sheet form, like metal panels that have been sent through a roller machine to produce thin sheets, or plywood panels that consist of thin layers of wood peeled off a log and then glued to each other with

---

[12] Drawing adapted from C. H. Waddington, "The Character of Biological Form," in *Aspects of Form*, edited by L. L. Whyte, Indiana University Press, 1966, p. 53.

[13] A space frame is a three-dimensional array of tetrahedrons, permitting it to be stable in all dimensions.

alternating grain directions. These sheet materials act as enclosing skins, while they also act structurally by resisting deformation in their plane and thus can be used, like braces, to stiffen a frame structure. By attaching a sheet material along its edges to the frame members, you achieve a structure wherein the posts of the frame can handle the compression forces while the beams handle the loads applied along their lengths, and the planar shear panels keep the frame from distorting and tipping over.

It is remarkable how much stiffening can be obtained from very thin and rather weak sheet materials—gypsum board, for example. Even paper can demonstrate a high resistance to deformation in its plane, especially when attached to a frame. A kite retains its shape in the wind due to the paper, firmly held to its planar shape by the tension string and the gently bowed wood frame.

Sheet materials basically resist tension and, like long, thin posts, buckle when compressed. Use a piece of paper to remind yourself of this fact. Sheet materials must be secured to the frame along their entire edge because they will be asked to resist tension coming from all directions. When the sheared frame shown below is pushed to the left, the material resists tension from the upper left to the lower right, but when the frame is pushed to the right, the material needs to resist tension from the upper right to the lower left. It can only do this if it is firmly attached to the frame at all its edges.

A shear panel firmly attached to a frame building can be thought of as a vertical beam, resisting displacement of the whole frame either left or right. Like a beam, it is more effective the shorter and deeper it is.

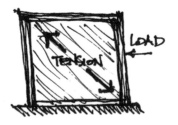 

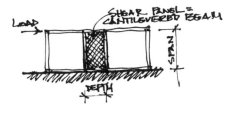

Typically, the walls of a wooden building are designed to act as shear panels. The aggregate ability of these walls to resist wind or earthquake forces from any direction is an important structural consideration. The fewer walls that exist in either direction, the stronger they must be. The architect will often hear the structural engineer comment that the developing design has plenty of shear walls in this direction but a limited amount in the other, and compensating measures will be required—typically strengthening those walls in the "weak" direction.

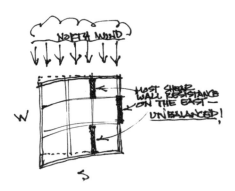

The shear walls must also be distributed across the floor plan in a balanced way such that a strong wind on a north wall, say, won't cause more deformation of the west walls than of the east walls. This can be illustrated in the plan view of the building (left).

FOLDED PLATES, SHELLS, AND SPACE FRAMES

Structures are endlessly interesting in their forms, yet they can generally be thought of as variations on the characteristics of simple stalks, skins, stone, and mud. Paper—a skin—resists deformation in its plane, but when folded like a fan it starts to work like a beam, allowing it to span over an open space with the ridges in compression and the valleys in tension. Folded plate roofs are developments of this basically stable

form created by the folding of flat surfaces.

Stalks can also gain stability by being woven into any basket-like shape and then stiffened with a mud coating. When this basic form is translated into reinforcing steel bars encased in a thin layer of concrete, we get a thin-shell structure. Or the stalks can be so thoroughly triangulated together, not just in two dimensions but in three, that a stable volume can result. This approach is used to create space frames—structures so stable within themselves that they can span over large areas and can be supported at any of the joints. Space frames are also employed to create complex forms that can be sheathed with a skin of glass, as in many of the most dramatically shaped buildings we see today.

DURABILITY I: DETAILING TO RESIST THE ELEMENTS

So, we have described a building that is stable: strong and resilient, able to successfully withstand all kinds of loads by minor stretching and compressing, then returning to its original condition after the storm, all without deforming or moving permanently. But it will still require some additional qualities that are needed to permit it to endure over the long run and to age gracefully, not destructively.

Such a newly built, strong building can still decay prematurely unless it is carefully detailed to prevent structural damage by natural elements such as water and insects and, to a lesser extent, by endless wind, sun, and chemicals. Well-designed details, though usually a part of the "skin," are very important in protecting and maintaining the strength and integrity of the structural "bones" of a building. Water can rust steel, weakening metal connectors and reinforcement, leading to the total failure of a structure. Dampness can promote rot if it remains in or near wood elements, which will rob the wood of any structural strength. And water that is allowed to penetrate concrete can freeze in the winter and expand, eventually destroying the material. Water will, of course, frequently fall upon the skin of a building, but the key is to create open channels that allow it to drain away promptly after the inundation, and to make sure no water is trapped more permanently within the fabric of the structure.

The simplest broad measures one can take to prevent water damage are to slope the roof so that it can drain promptly, give it generous overhangs to minimize the amount of rain that strikes the walls, windows, and doors, and gather the roof runoff in gutters and downspouts and then lead it well away from the foundations.

Beyond this, the building must be detailed carefully to prevent water intrusion, particularly at the joints between surfaces. For this we usually employ sheet-metal flashing or, less desirably, caulk. Sheet metals such as galvanized steel (iron coated with zinc), copper, aluminum, and lead are rust-resistant and therefore used for flashing. They guide the water that strikes the building over and away from any joints or cracks in the skin of the building and prevent any water from penetrating and remaining in the crevices of the joints.

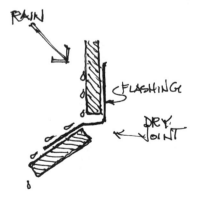

Any cracks in new, exposed concrete walls and foundations always need to be filled and sealed. Exposed concrete is often finish-coated with a water repellent, again to prevent small water pockets from freezing, forcing the concrete farther apart, creating a bigger pocket for the next rain and so on, until whole pieces of concrete break off from the main body of the concrete (spalling) or until the water eventually reaches the inner steel reinforcement and rust begins to destroy the structure's integrity.

Water destroys wood not by rust, of course, but by the promotion of rot by microorganisms that eat away at the material, leaving a soft, spongy, discolored area that is structurally useless. This doesn't occur when the wood is dry, or when it is fully submerged and wet; it occurs, rather, in the area between dry and wet, where the wood is trying to dry at one place but additional water is present in an adjacent area. A good example is a wooden pier in the water: Rot will occur only at the water line, not above or below. So when wood does get wet—either during a storm, due to a waterline leak, or due to the water vapor in the shower—the trick is to let it completely dry out afterward by allowing water to drain away and air to freely circulate around the wood to remove its excess humidity. The best current practice in the detailing of exterior wood siding, for example, is to create a shallow space between the wood siding or shingles and the inner water-repellent skin of the building by attaching the siding to batts or strips of wood. This allows any water that does get behind the siding to drain down to the ground freely. This space also allows air to circulate freely behind this wood siding to ensure full drying.

WET AIR

DRY AIR

This type of drainage wall, known as a rain screen, has another advantage in that the exterior skin is separated from the water-repellent building paper behind, intercepting the wind and taking the full wind pressure at the siding's exterior surface, thus reducing the pressure in the gap next to the building paper. This reduced pressure is then less likely to force water into and behind the building paper. Finally, the exterior siding keeps the direct sun off the building paper, extending its life considerably.

Trapped moisture in a wood structure is eventually fatal (to the building). Moisture can get into the walls of a building from penetration through the outer waterproofing layer, or from a leak in the piping inside the walls. Actually, the wood typically used to initially build is "wet"—as much as 30 to 40 percent water—and it is expected that the wood will gradually dry out to the average ambient air humidity, typically around 10 percent. But if the walls are sealed on both sides with vapor barriers that prevent water vapor from exiting the wet interior, a perfect damp condition is perpetuated that ensures rot. The walls must breathe, constantly adjusting the inner wood's humidity to the dryer air outside and/or inside.

Then there is the water vapor situation that can create such confusion among designers and builders and can potentially cause extensive rot damage to the structural wood inside frame walls. In a cold climate, the water vapor that is part of the warm, high-humidity air in the kitchen or shower will migrate into the wall cavity, where it will eventually condense into liquid water on the inside of the very cold exterior siding. The problem is that a vapor barrier was probably installed under the exterior siding by the contractor, perhaps guided by the architect's drawing. But this vapor barrier prevents the humid water vapor from passing to the outside, trapping it in the wall cavity, where the water vapor condenses into water, also trapped in the cavity. In this climate, it's finally becoming common practice to place the vapor barrier under the interior drywall or plaster, not behind the exterior siding.

The situation is reversed in a warm, humid climate where the air in the house is chilled by an air conditioner for basic comfort. The warm water vapor from the outside air enters the wall cavity from the outside, and if it encounters a very cool interior surface, such as a vapor barrier under the drywall, it will condense, leaving water in the wall cavity, again producing rot. In such a climate, the vapor barrier should be placed under the exterior siding.

Wood has another natural enemy; namely, termites that eat the wood, leaving nothing but sawdust behind. Termites live in the dirt below the building and seek out wood that can be reached within 6 to 8 inches above the dirt. Once the termites reach any wood near the dirt, they eat their way up the wooden member, potentially getting into every piece of attached wood. Wood must therefore be kept well up above the ground, either upon a concrete foundation or a metal support. Wood can, however, be made more termite- and rot-proof by being pressure treated with a preservative, usually containing some compounds of copper. The hesitation in using pressure-treated wood is that its protection isn't perfect, and the preservative—poisonous if ingested—eventually leaches out into the soil, harming the natural organisms in the soil.

So the structural firmness of a building is not just a matter of strength on day one, but in the long term rests upon careful detailing by the architect, ensuring conditions that preserve the strength of the materials and prevent their decay over time.

DURABILITY II: PATINA AND REPAIR

To this point we have described *firmitas* as an inherent property of the completed building, perhaps giving the impression that the building's ability to resist the forces of nature over time is the sole responsibility of its designers and builders. But regardless of the quality of design, materials, and construction, buildings, like all things, will age. They require ongoing maintenance and occasional repair by their owners and inhabitants.

Greek stone houses, for example, demand annual whitewashing to fill tiny gaps and holes in the masonry before they become larger and start to invite water in, threatening the integrity of the wall. Almost all roof materials require periodic replacement, with the possible exception of clay and concrete tiles. Exterior paint must be renewed every few years. Gutters, door and window hardware, and mechanical equipment all need attention at various times. The forces of nature continue to bear on man-made buildings, at first creating a patina of wear, then gradually affecting the ability of the building's elements to function properly. Although it is true that *firmitas* may initially be ample, from the day that owners and residents start using the building it becomes their responsibility to maintain and repair. From this point on, the usefulness of the building will entail attention to its firmness— *firmitas* and *utilitas* begin to interact.

If buildings aren't carefully designed, don't age well, and can't be gradually repaired and maintained, they will eventually decay, require demolition, and need to be replaced with new construction. In this sense, they lack the durability and sustainability aspects of *firmitas*.

Our consumer-focused society seems to have become accustomed to the rapid obsolescence of resource-intensive products, appliances, and electronics. The tendency is to throw away toasters, TVs, computers, and cell phones because they can no longer be easily and economically repaired. Many of our buildings have come to suffer this same fate. One early example is the radiant-heated slab floors of the 1950s and 1960s that used copper piping in the concrete slab to carry the circulating hot water. This worked well until any leak developed in some part of the metal tubing: To repair this would require breaking up a good portion of the floor slab to find the leak, which essentially meant breaking up the foundation of the house.

Features that are designed to permit and encourage ongoing repair include access to plumbing and wiring connections, use of screws in place of nails, and limited size and weight of building components that can be put in place by hand rather than a crane. Painted wooden windows and doors do require periodic repainting, but at least they can be renewed in this way, whereas aluminum windows and doors are attacked by salts and acids in the atmosphere and can't be refinished—after several years they simply require replacement. Natural wood interior finishes can absorb an almost infinite amount of use, absorbing the inevitable knocks, scratches, and stains over the years, and still retain their inherent organic and natural appearance. This isn't true of highly finished materials, such as polished metal, that often show every mark of use, marks that detract from the installed finish.

In general, a building that is composed of highly refined materials and finishes will show the normal marks of usage in a more unattractive way than a building composed of more relaxed and informal finishes. A normally warped ceiling beam will appear natural in a rustic building, but will appear as an expensive and unrepairable defect in a modernistic, clean, "minimal" structure. The buildings of the modern architecture movement (those of the early 20th century) were especially subject to this form of poor aging. Instead of thick, overgenerous walls and hefty, frequently spaced ceiling beams, modern architecture called for thin glassy walls with minimal structural posts and exposed ceiling beams. When finished, these buildings radiated a fresh, lean, airy feeling of elegance. But after a relatively short period the weathering on the exterior wood beams and the small but inevitable warping of the minimized ceiling beams began to create an impression of excessive frailty. A warped beam in a rustic building is charming—in a modern building, where precision is the goal, it is seen as a defect, and

one that can't easily be repaired. The 1950s–1960s period of California homebuilding included clean, affordable, elegant modern homes designed by noted Bay Area architects and built by the developer Eichler (drawing facing page). These homes depended on the materials of construction remaining true and straight, a difficult request for long, widely spaced lengths of post and beam.

One of modern architecture's great shortcomings is that its buildings do not typically assume an attractive patina over the years, but instead often fail to maintain the pristine perfection that the stripped-down aesthetic demands. These buildings most often look best the day they are finished and begin their gradual decline from that day on; in this sense, they do not possess complete *firmitas*.

REDUNDANCY AND SUSTAINABILITY: REMODELING AND ADAPTATION

We began this chapter on *firmitas* by pointing out that the lifespan of buildings in highly urbanized areas is getting shorter and shorter, creating a waste of energy and resources that we can increasingly ill afford. The typical problem isn't that buildings are structurally deficient—indeed, the wrecking ball is often pulling down perfectly good materials to be replaced with similarly good materials. Steel, concrete, and even wood will not wear out over time if water can be kept away from them to prevent rust, freezing, and rot. Rather, buildings are increasingly replaced with new buildings because they can't adapt to the changing demands for more space, different kinds of space, or a fresher "look"—either the replacement of materials that have aged unattractively or the replacement of the entire building with a more contemporary style.

When the inhabitants and owners want to expand, reconfigure, or remodel their building in order to maintain its usefulness, the building should be able to accommodate these changes. The building will need to be more than firm: It will need to be structurally redundant. It must have more strength than originally needed in order to permit future changes: additional loads, fewer walls, or openings cut into floors. If the building cannot withstand such modifications, even with some reasonable structural compensation, it will be sold or replaced with new construction.

Buildings are often torn down to be replaced with much larger structures, and this is typically due to increasing density and land values. Big, aggressive institutions like university campuses or large hospital complexes have an ongoing appetite for building more facilities, and the surrounding neighborhoods—often residential—get slowly gobbled up. Perfectly good houses and apartment buildings give way to large research or medical buildings. Once in a blue moon the owner of a small property that lies in the path of an expanding institution refuses to sell out regardless of the offered price, creating amusing contrasts in scale and use.

This is not a new phenomenon, and great cities share this history of structurally sound buildings being replaced with larger ones. Sometimes, though, the smaller building can be saved by being moved as a unit to an empty site elsewhere.

Another approach is to design a building with the capacity to expand at a later date if necessary. This is most economically done by enlarging the footprint of the building on its own lot rather than by adding to it vertically. But

modest vertical additions to well-built buildings—those with some structural redundancy—can often be done with relatively modest reinforcement of the stiffness of the lower walls and modifications to the foundation.

The most typical approach to saving an existing building is via re-modeling: changing the configuration of the various rooms and circulation paths, removing some walls and even floor areas to open up some areas, and adding new walls to create additional small spaces. The city's old industrial buildings thus get transformed into offices, restaurants, even housing, saving money, energy, and material resources. A more dramatic approach to preserving those buildings that are structurally sound is to build over them, leaving them in place but adding supporting columns just outside their walls.

Perhaps the most eloquent and insightful book on the subject of adaptability of buildings is *How Buildings Learn: What Happens after They're Built*, by Stewart Brand (Penguin, 1995). To reduce the waste of energy and materials incurred in the replacement of old buildings with new, Brand distinguishes between two main approaches: the High Road (building for the ages with the most permanent materials and the most sturdy structure) and the Low Road (temporary buildings designed for certain change, with good enough materials that can be repurposed). A memorial might appropriately be done in the High Road style, whereas the temporary barracks built during World War II are good examples of Low Road building. As late as the 1960s such barracks were being successfully used as grad student offices at the University of California at Berkeley. They were well built and sturdy but absolutely basic and straightforward. Brand offers a series of wise suggestions for doing good Low Road buildings: Make the buildings rectangular to permit future additions; use long-lived, quality materials that can be re-used; and substitute screws, nuts, and bolts for nails to permit the disassembly and re-use of those materials.

We now confront a future that necessitates conservation and on-going repair if we are to sustain our planet. This demands a more expansive vision of *firmitas* that offers not only safety but also resilience, not only long life but also adaptability, and not only a structure that shapes our lives but also one that gives us the opportunity for creative new directions.

PSYCHOLOGICAL FIRMNESS: INTERACTIONS BETWEEN *FIRMITAS* AND *VENUSTAS*

This brings us ultimately to the issue of psychological firmness, the feeling or perception that a building is strong and durable, quite apart from the question of whether it actually is. Contemporary high-rise buildings are increasingly safe, as the codes and structural engineering knowledge imbue them with extraordinary ability to withstand earthquakes and strong wind loads. These very tall buildings are now designed with an ability to withstand the very largest probable loads and forces of nature safely.[14] They are designed to respond to these loads by yielding slightly in a modest and safe manner, then returning to their original position. But in a very tall building this response may be a vibrating oscillation that amounts to several feet, back and forth, until it gradually dies down. This may be perfectly safe for the integrity of the building itself, but it may be hugely unsettling to the inhabitants of these upper floors. After the massive 2011 earthquake in Japan, many inhabitants of residential high-rises in Japan decided that the fear generated by these big sideways oscillations was not worth the good views, and they quit their leases and moved to low-rise accommodations. This exodus from high-rise units caused a difficult economic situation, with many empty, unsellable units in these new high-rises. The buildings are structurally sound, but not psychologically sound.

Psychological firmness can stem from the mere appearance of the building—thick walls of heavy masonry will appear firmer and stronger than thin walls of glass and metal columns, regardless of whether the building is safe from collapse in an earthquake or not. The experience of past structural failures has taught us that, in fact, buildings

---

[14] They are not, however, designed to withstand extraordinary and improbable events such as the assault on the World Trade Center towers.

of heavy masonry can be especially prone to collapse unless they are adequately reinforced, whereas lightly framed buildings can be made to yield safely without failure, aided by their lower mass.

The feeling that a building is firm and durable can also come from its shape, how it appears to sit on the ground. A building that has a wide base on the lower floors and gets narrower as it gets higher will appear stable and safe. This stems from our physical experience of piling things up—sand, dishes, and leaves. This feeling is reinforced by our knowledge of historical buildings that follow this pattern. Similarly, we will feel that a building is firm if its cantilevers are modest, again based on our sympathetic feeling for the forces within the structure.

But contemporary structural-steel engineering enables architects to create buildings that appear to ignore structural soundness. These adventuresome designs can be made to be structurally sound, but part of what makes them exciting is that they don't appear to be so. This visual flirtation with danger is stimulating and interesting, though often one is willing to visit such a structure but not to "live" there. In the case of the 2012 China Central Television office building by Rem Koolhaas (below), it isn't even clear that one would feel comfortable going inside. Two separate towers are each capped with huge cantilevers that link up to form a bent bridge 13 stories above the ground.

This form is obviously a structural "stretch," an unprecedented form that requires a complex structural solution, which is in fact expressed in the external diagonal bracing. How comfortable would one feel up in the cantilevered corner, or directly under it on the plaza at the base? In another of his buildings, his earlier Dutch Embassy in Berlin, Koolhaas confronts us

with a major glass-floored corridor 30 feet above the ground that leads into the building. Some visitors will simply not walk across it.

In spite of the beautiful materials and detailing of these buildings, and in spite of the great novelty and interest they create in their urban contexts, they exemplify provocative, aggressive architecture by creating a kind of "psychological *in-firmitas*." Koolhaas asks us to confront our perceptions of structural stability, and perhaps intends us to get a kick out of his somewhat threatening spaces, a bit like the thrill we can get on a rollercoaster.

But the flip side of the "psychological *in-firmitas*" coin is a possible positive aesthetic response to a building's structure. We may experience the structural aspect of a building as being beautiful, interesting, even spiritually moving. Quite apart from a building's colors and textures, its spaces and views, its functions and comforts, we may have a significant aesthetic response to our perception of its structure, of how it handles the various forces that nature places upon it.

Take bridges, for example, structures that aside from their primary function of spanning distances are rather similar to buildings. Most bridges invite aesthetic appreciation of their structural achievement—the Brooklyn Bridge and the Golden Gate Bridge are universally judged to be beautiful and exciting, but even more modest New England covered bridges stir strong aesthetic responses. What are we responding to? We think it is the clear intentions of the design, a focus on the structural necessities, an attention to economy of means, providing just what is required and eliminating the unnecessary, an omission of the irrelevant. We see the similarity between the engineers' technique and nature's methods.

Consider the 1890 Firth of Forth Bridge in Scotland, one of the first all-iron bridges and a very carefully engineered structure. Its design was novel and controversial at the time, based on cantilevered arms extending out on both sides of the piers standing in the water, arms that support straight intermediate sections.

To explain the structural strategy that was being proposed, the designers illustrated the concept using human actors, two taking the roles of the double cantilever sections, a third being supported in the middle by the cantilevered trusses. By putting ourselves in their shoes, we can begin to "feel" and thus understand the forces within the bridge's members: This is how we can derive aesthetic pleasure from a building's structure too. Without a detailed knowledge of engineering, we can observe the structural elements and how they are working together, and can relate almost directly to their structural roles as if our own bodies were doing the spanning.

The 20th-century architectural critic Geoffrey Scott argued in *The Architecture of Humanism* (Norton, 1914) that great architecture invites us to identify personally with the building, to feel almost physically in our own bodies the building's lines, masses, and spaces, as though we are that building and might thus sense what the building is feeling. This seems quite right to us, and is why we illustrated physical forces with human forms earlier in this chapter. We empathize with the work of the maidens supporting the roof of the Erectheum porch in Athens: Looking at the structure, we too feel we are supporting the roof.

The architect Forrest Wilson has dramatically illustrated the forces

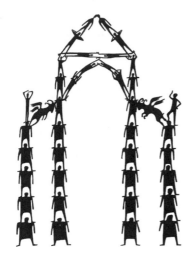

in a buttressed Gothic arch by showing how a gang of gymnasts (and a couple of rams) could form such a structure simply using their bodies (drawing at left). The wooden roof structure consists of top compression rafters tied into a stable triangle with a couple of tension guys. This wooden roof truss bears down directly onto the inner vertical piers, with the central vault above pushing outward, requiring compensating inward thrust—here provided by a couple of rams. They in turn push the tops of the buttresses outward, and that is compensated with added weight atop them, making it more difficult to overturn them. And we see how the pressure inside the stone columns and buttresses increases as one moves downward, each man becoming larger to support all those above him.

THE ROLE OF STRUCTURAL EXPRESSION IN ARCHITECTURE

As mentioned earlier, architects rarely if ever do their own structural design and calculations any more. For reasons of liability, difficulty of calculation, and a lack of specialized structural experience, an architect almost always teams up with a structural engineer, who in the best of cases will be an active member of the design team from beginning to end, giving guidance all the way through, from the early stages of design to the supervision of the actual construction. Gone are the days of the Renaissance architect who was the master of engineering, design, decoration and construction.

But it's also becoming evident that something important has been lost as a result of this specialization, in the architect's stepping back from structural responsibility and the public's hesitation in learning more about it. An overreliance on the engineer's ability to make any architectural design "work," to be structurally firm, has led in many cases to the design of buildings that are structurally "difficult"—yes, they may work formally and functionally, but sometimes at a great expense in structural compensation for the adventurous designs. Some contemporary designs appear structurally irrational, and intentionally so, perhaps to engage our curiosity and wonder that such a building could be built. In the hands of some architects, this structural bravado can be truly exciting.

For example, Frank Gehry's design for the Walt Disney Concert Hall in Los Angeles is a stunning piece of architecture, and most visitors feel that it is appropriate for its location and purpose. But the actual structural framework of the building, which in itself is a marvel of design and manufacturing, is totally hidden beneath the shiny metal curves of its skin, preventing a full understanding and appreciation of the overall reality of this work.[15] We can really enjoy the freedom of the shapes, the glamour of the shiny metal skin, and the perfection and warmth of the concert auditorium. But this hidden, almost secretive aspect of the structure introduces a counter note, a subtle

---

[15] Unlike Gehry's earlier Barcelona Fish sculpture, in which the visible supporting structure is an integral part of the work.

kind of alienation, by implying that we aren't fully part of the culture that creates these puzzling dramatic creations.

Another example of a building that seems to flout structural logic is the recently completed New Museum of Contemporary Art in Manhattan by the firm SANAA, where each successive floor is offset from the underlying one (drawing below). This building form may have some functional reasoning behind it (the provision of daylight to the interior, for instance), and some may find that it presents an interesting and attractive appearance, but one may well question its blatant expression of a difficult structural assembly.

We are seeing more buildings that seem to defy conventional structural logic. Some of this is due to new materials (plastics, carbon-fiber) and to existing materials like glass that can now be made to work structurally. But the biggest reason is the power of the computer in the hands of designers who want to create new, unprecedented forms. With the computer one can trace the contours of any shape, record the data for use by other structural computer programs, execute any required drawings for permit and construction, and directly provide the data that machines can use to manufacture the many individual and unique physical elements that are required for the structure.

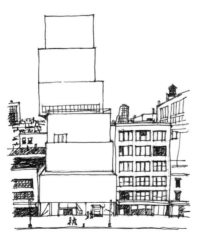

Students are often influenced by these structurally daring examples, encouraged by them to downplay or even ignore more traditional and "rational" structural approaches in favor of dramatic gestures designed mostly to grab one's attention. We feel it's important that students be encouraged to incorporate obvious structural considerations into their projects, as well as explore more innovative forms. What is potentially lost by this structural adventurousness, however, is a cultural appreciation for the added cost of structure and difficulty of building these dramatic buildings. What's also lost is the aesthetic opportunity to express structural truths, the natural flow of forces, and the means by which buildings resist loads.

This aesthetic role of structure will be discussed further in Chapter 5 on *venustas*, but here we suggest that an empathetic, intuitive recognition of how a building's structure works can help us to relate to it with understanding, confidence, and, in some cases, awe. These reactions can be the basis of a positive aesthetic response. But if the building defies our ability to "feel" or understand its structural strategy, we won't be as confidently open to its fuller messages of appropriate function and beauty.

Of course, there can be a flush of pleasure in being seduced by a new building's novelty, complexity, daring, and expense. We architects are especially prone to this initial charge of interest and excitement produced by the latest feats of the current architectural stars. But this kind of pleasure can quickly fade. Novelty demands fresh novelty, rendering last year's building, well, last year. There is such a thing as aesthetic durability—the building should age well—and one can well wonder which of today's computer-aided buildings will stand the test of time.

And so, we conclude this chapter with a structurally innovative building that we think will indeed remain compelling and satisfying over time. We refer to the 1980 Thorncrown Chapel in Eureka Springs, Arkansas, designed by E. Fay Jones (see p. 142).

This building is composed of long, light wood elements, woven together in a completely transparent fashion, enabling us to vividly see and mentally grasp the order of structural posts, rafters, and trusslike smaller members—and, above all, the role of triangles in stiffening the whole building. Beyond its many additional virtues, like harmonizing with the landscape, the structure itself is a major contributor to our sense of the chapel's beauty.

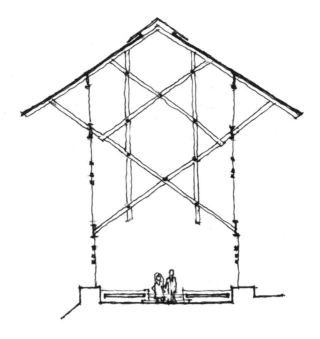

We all know that contemporary life involves stress, anxiety, and unpredictability and that our culture must include a recognition of these realities. Need this reality be expressed in the very structure of today's new buildings? A client who seeks a novel structure, something that will be instantly recognizable as a brand, an icon of style, prestige, and wealth, may certainly welcome the drama of a design that appears to defy structural logic. But that client who values his or her investment will not entertain a structural adventure that entails unnecessary risk. "Give us something that looks structurally precarious (for fun and excitement), but make sure it isn't."

It is true that life is full of disorder and confusing events, but it is equally true that we still live in our skin, with our feet on the ground, part of the living earth. We propose that the structure of the tree outside our window provides a profound and valid example of how we can build. It's not just the deep spreading roots, the decreasing thickness of the trunk as it ascends, the thickening of material at the joints between branches, the overall symmetry of the spreading crown, and the flexibility of the whole tree in response to wind. Besides these basic structural characteristics, we recognize the importance of long-term responses to environmental forces—the growing toward the main source of light, the leaning away from the predominant winds, the growth around a permanent rock outcropping, adapting and repairing its form over time. Last, the tree is in balance with its site, returning rain to the earth for later consumption and shading it to minimize evaporation. The tree will be stable, able to withstand and adjust to new stresses, and will thrive in its ground, enjoying long life. Let our building structures do no less. □

"The first principle of architectural beauty is that the essential lines of a construction be determined by a perfect appropriateness to its use."

—GUSTAVE EIFFEL, 1887

"Good buildings don't just fulfill existing functions, they suggest new ones."

—WITOLD RYBCZYNSKI, 2013

UTILITAS
The Usefuln
tecture

CHAPTER FOUR

UTILITAS:
The Usefulness of Architecture

IN THE LAST CHAPTER on *firmitas* we saw how the structures we build respond to the earth, how they endure the constantly varying forces of nature. In this chapter on *utilitas* we will explore how these structures must also respond to humankind, to our ever-changing capacities, needs, desires, and foibles. And we will see how people, in turn, respond to those built structures.

The foremost human need satisfied by our built structures is basic bodily protection from the forces of nature: weather, gravity, and predators. Architecture accommodates those bodily needs in several ways: by tempering climatic extremes, by ensuring safety from intruders, and by providing spaces that fit the dimensions and capacities of our body. It not only serves to temper the climate but also offers a range of options that allow us to adjust our immediate environment, our microclimate, by providing openable windows, sheltered courtyards, and sunny and shaded rooms. The structures we build provide protection from intruders by offering both solid enclosure and visual connection through window openings that act as watchful eyes on the entries. And architecture must also ensure physical accessibility by allowing people at all stages of life—children, adults, and the elderly—to negotiate stairs, ramps, and entries in order to easily access all the spaces of a building.

Once physical survival and a degree of physical comfort have been achieved, our environment must then aid in satisfying our longer-term living strategies and procedures: How might we shape and organize our spaces so that we can better cook, sleep, build, repair, meet, and barter? Attention to *utilitas* helps us to arrange the flow of people, tasks, and materials so that we can effectively carry out our activities and duties. *Utilitas* means that our built spaces function well for us— they "work"—thus adding a wealth of benefits to our cities, businesses, and homes. For instance, a well-designed factory is more productive, whereas a well-designed shopping street offers a full range of services that people need while shopping: convenient parking or bus stops, the required variety of stores and shops, along with a lunch spot. A well-designed house supports our needs to cook, sleep, and work.

Not only must the structures we design function in ways that address our survival and everyday needs, they can also be shaped to satisfy our psychological needs and desires and our often complex emotions and feelings. Having provided for actual physical survival and security, for example, we also want to *feel* safe and secure. One does not necessarily follow from the other, as a ride in a glass-walled elevator can illustrate. Psychological matters are complex. They include our desires on the one hand for privacy and individual self-expression and on the other for social togetherness and a sense of belonging. One of the most critical functions a built space can provide is the opportunity for each person to find a satisfying balance between privacy and social interaction, between individual and group work, and between reflection and conversation. These psychological needs include options for choice, varieties of experience, and simply the freedom to be ourselves.

Finally, architecture may be functional in a deeper way, by offering an emotional feeling of solace and peace, a sense we are at home in the world in spite of our occasional difficulties. A church or temple, a memorial or monument, even a museum, can work to elevate our thoughts and feelings to a higher level. Some spatial experiences can encourage us to forget for a moment our own bodily and psychological needs, and to give us an inner sense of our place in the universe. The Vietnam Veterans Memorial on the Mall in Washington, D.C., is a powerful example of the effect a certain kind of spatial experience can have on our emotional 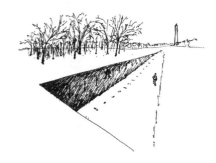 relationship to tragic events like the war in Vietnam. Designed by the architect Maya Lin in 1981, the memorial is essentially a long wall of polished black granite incised with the names of those who died in the war. The dark reflective surface of the wall acts as a mirror, in which visitors see their own faces as they read the soldiers' names listed in the order each was killed. The wall follows a path that slopes down into the earth, making it seem to grow higher and higher. The path then turns abruptly and rises up again in the direction of the obelisk of the Washington Monument. Visitors to the memorial often describe feeling a strong connection with the reality and horrors of war and the terrible loss of life it causes. It functions well as a memorial; it also does so beautifully—but that is the topic of the next chapter.

So as we begin to explore the concept of *utilitas* it is helpful to remember that architecture can be useful to us in these four major ways: the way it fits, protects, and comforts our body; the way it facilitates and enriches our desired activities; the way it responds to our psychological needs and emotions; and the way it engages and expresses our intellectual and spiritual sides. We are also learning that we need to add a fifth function: In order for architecture to continue to be useful to us in the future, it must not destroy the environment. Instead of depleting resources, our buildings will need to replenish them.

We don't want to make the mistake, however, of thinking that architecture can always fit our needs like a glove. Once built, architecture is relatively fixed and static, whereas its many users vary enormously in their individual needs and goals. Furthermore, each individual's needs and goals are constantly changing—from moment to moment as well as over the course of a lifetime. The paradoxical attempt to create long-lasting durable spaces to fit the ever-changing desires of their many users is one of the central challenges in creating architecture.

Similarly, we need to ask, "*Utilitas* for whom?" Architecture serves not only the actual users, current and future, but also the larger context: the clients and institutions that create it, the developers who hope to profit from it, as well as the neighborhoods and cities that host it. Each of these interested parties has differing needs that the architecture must address, and often these needs conflict with one another: The hospital's need for control and efficiency, for example, may not harmonize with the patient's need for calm and rest. Nor can we ignore the sense in which architecture serves the needs of the architect, for livelihood, ego satisfaction, and peer recognition. Nevertheless, *utilitas*, in the best case, tries to satisfy as many of these conflicting goals and needs as possible. But before we dive into the heart of the role of *utilitas* in architecture today, let's review what Vitruvius had to say about it 2,000 years ago.

VITRUVIUS'S NOTION OF *UTILITAS*

Vitruvius specified that all departments of architecture (which for him included not only buildings but also timepieces and machinery) needed to be built with an eye focused equally on durability, convenience, and beauty. For him, *utilitas* meant:

> When the arrangement of the apartments is faultless and presents no hindrance to use, and when each class of building is assigned to its suitable and appropriate exposure.[1]

---

[1] *Vitruvius: The Ten Books of Architecture*, translated by Morris Hicky Morgan, Dover Press, 1960, p. 17.

Or, from a more recent translation:

> The principle of utility will be observed if the design allows faultless unimpeded use through the disposition of the spaces and the allocation of each type of space is properly oriented, appropriate, and comfortable.[2]

Thus, we see that Vitruvius emphasized two of the important aspects of utility: the facilitation of our varied activities and bodily comfort. Let's start with his ideas about how to build with the body and its health in mind.

Vitruvius recommends that buildings be oriented to the sun and wind to minimize any excessive temperatures and breezes. Working in a world without modern air-conditioning, it is not surprising that he places as much emphasis on climatic factors (which are now re-emerging as a central architectural concern under the rubric of "sustainability") as upon proper arrangement of rooms. He emphasizes choice of a healthy site with much detailed discussion of how to lay out walls and streets to prevent exposure to "detrimental winds."

Vitruvius thought that cities themselves were best located in temperate, moderate climates, high above marshes, and not exposed to excessively harsh sunlight. Coming from northern Italy, he was leery of southern and western exposures to the sun during the warmest period of the day, feeling that excessive heat weakens and softens one, an unhealthy condition in his mind. He conceived of the body as composed of the four elements—earth, air, heat, and moisture—and felt that the body's composition would be the healthiest when these elements were in balance, a balance that could be upset by too much exposure to any of them. We need not agree with his view of our bodies' composition, but we can agree that one of architecture's goals is to help give us fresh air and a comfortable range of temperature and dryness. As an example of his advice to prevent excessive winds throughout the city,

---

[2] *Vitruvius: Ten Books on Architecture*, translated by Ingrid Rowland, Cambridge University Press, 1999, p. 26.

he suggests orienting the streets at an angle to the prevailing winds so that the walls serve as a partial barrier to the breeze. His specific advice needs to be applied judiciously depending on the climate and locale, but his attention to the effect of the sun and winds on the living environment is especially critical today.

Turning to his instructions for adapting structures and spaces to their intended use, he states that the arrangement of spaces, inside and out, must be laid out in accordance with the needs and habits of the people using them so that no awkwardness is imposed on them, and that these spaces must not make their use difficult. Different types of buildings, each type accommodating a different kind of activity, should also be located in a way that is the most useful and appropriate in response to both the needs of that particular type as well as the qualities of the place.

Vitruvius deals with how the arrangement of spaces, buildings, and the rooms within needs to correspond to the intended activities they are serving, in harmony with the expected social and cultural norms of the specific society. He deals with the proper types of houses for different levels and occupations of the owners, the arrangement of rooms to accommodate guests, different home businesses, and the distinction between public parts of the house, where unexpected visitors can enter, and private rooms, where no one would enter without an invitation. He talks about the provision of varied spaces for dining, dealing with the fact that men and women ate separately, and that multiple dining areas needed to be provided for comfort during the various seasons. He discusses the orientation of rooms and the location of their windows to admit the appropriate kind of light for each different type of room: cool eastern light for a bedroom that will be used in the morning or for a library to preserve books, and warmer southern light for an olive oil storage room to keep the oil from solidifying. A northern orientation is appropriate for a summer dining room, picture gallery, workroom, or painter's studio, both for coolness and for steady light that allows colors to be worked with in an unchanging light quality.

In the design of outdoor forums, he tells us that they need to be rectangular, not square, to enable gladiator demonstrations, and should be sized in proportion to the population to prevent either overcrowding or empty, unused space. The forum should be surrounded with shops, businesses, a bank, government offices, toilets, and a gallery, all to add vitality and life to the public forum. He also specifies that the layout of a theater emerges from the need of the audience to see and hear the action on the stage, and must offer adequate straight and clear exit routes to prevent crowd jams at the end of the performance. In several cases he makes specific suggestions for how to accomplish all of these requirements.

Two thousand years later we recognize that Vitruvius covered many of the essentials of *utilitas*, and it is clear that we must continue to work with all the aspects that he set out. But as we know, the world and how we live in it are always changing. How have these essentials of *utilitas* evolved in ways that make them appropriate for our needs now? We'll begin with the physical aspects of *utilitas*, the ways that architecture protects and fits our bodies.

THERMAL BALANCE AND COMFORT

Among all our changing needs and desires, we share one physical constant: Our bodies continually attempt to maintain an internal temperature of 98.6°F regardless of the exterior climate. By a wonderful variety of strategies, like shivering, which increases the heat generated by muscles to compensate for cold weather, and perspiring, which cools the skin through evaporation in hot weather, we can maintain a feeling of relative comfort in almost any surrounding. Our bodies are also constantly making involuntary internal adjustments, like breathing and blood circulation rate, as well as voluntary adjustments in our level of activity or moving to a more comfortable place.

We can extend our ability to balance our temperature with clothing, bundling up for skiing, stripping down for swimming. But these strategies have their limits, and architecture is able to extend these limits to our thermal comfort. In cold weather, enclosed interior and sheltered exterior spaces can offer protection from the wind and be warmed by the inhabitants' bodies, incoming sunlight, and fire. In hot weather, semi-enclosed interior and sheltered exterior spaces can encourage ventilation, cooling the breezes by passing them over evaporative pools, and shading the users from the hot, direct sun.

Thermal comfort is an important aspect of architecture because it is a prerequisite for all our everyday activities. When we directly sense that a place is too hot or cold, we can't do much there that is enjoyable or worthwhile. In more severe climates, architecture can literally save our lives by preventing death from freezing or heat stroke.

When we physically work hard, we generate more internal heat than we need; we start to get too hot and wish we could move to a cooler spot. And when we sit down to read quietly, our internal heat production slows down and we may feel too cool and, to compensate, we might seek out a warmer spot. But an artificially controlled and unchanging climate such as we find in a shopping mall or an office building, though it's meant to provide a pleasant environment, can in reality create several challenges to our

thermal comfort. First, the interior uniform climate, lacking a variation of some cooler and some warmer spaces, can actually prevent us
from being able to find comfort as our activities change.[3] Second, we
can often receive an unpleasant shock when we leave the artificial interior climate inside a building to venture outdoors; our body struggles
to adjust so quickly to such an extreme difference between inside and
out. Third, this rigid control of interior temperature is expensive, increasing power demands, which is damaging to the environment. Last,
an unchanging interior climate can deaden any pleasure we might
receive from the periodic stimulus of a refreshing breath of air, a dap-
pling of light and shade, or the gentle mist of a fountain spray.

In her inspiring book *Thermal Delight in Architecture* (MIT Press,
1979), Lisa Heschong describes how a concern for thermal balance and
comfort can be a primary driver of architectural design. She illumi-
nates the thermal wisdom of the heavy mass of adobe buildings in the
Southwest, and the delicate, lightweight, and permeable structures of
the tropics.

Traditionally, architecture shaped itself in response to the climate,
not just to preserve its own structural integrity but also to serve its
users by providing a tempered, comfortable thermal environment.
Throughout the 20th century, however, cheaper energy enabled indoor
thermal comfort to be provided by mechanical air-conditioning rather
than the fabric of the building itself. A new consciousness of how our
energy use is threatening the whole environment has led to awareness
of the harmful effects of excessive energy use and a reversal of this
trend. "Green" buildings offer thermal comfort via proper orientation
to the sun, interior thermal storage, better insulation and infiltration
control, and appropriate solar shading. Instead of a total reliance on
mechanical air-conditioning, sustainable architecture involves a
more relaxed response to thermal control—by letting the interior tem-

---

[3] Most modern air-conditioned buildings do not have individually openable windows. They would complicate totally
uniform temperature control, but would facilitate individual adjustment of comfort.

perature vary a bit in response to the outside temperature and the production of heat on the interior. Future buildings will increasingly give the users some individual control over their immediate environment via openable windows, adjustable shading, and individual thermostats.

This element of individual control is a key to creating thermally comfortable architectural spaces. Spaces that provide a variety of microclimates allow users to find their own best spot, permitting them to make their own adjustments to the environment. A sunny courtyard is improved by shade trees and a fountain, a patio table by an adjustable umbrella, and an interior workstation by an openable window and operable shades.

Urban density also plays a role in the creation of thermal comfort. Mid-rise row houses, for example, are easier to keep warm and cool than single detached dwellings: Each unit is partially insulated from outside temperature extremes by its neighbors to the sides, above, and below (drawing below). The thermal mass of the group of units (relative to its surface area) evens out the daily temperature extremes.

A dense city must, however, deal with the problem caused by a lack of open green space to help cool the streets and facades in summer. Many cities have been addressing this issue by retrofitting buildings with rooftop gardens. These gardens offer refreshing oases and views, providing relief from the stuffy interior spaces and also helping to prevent overheating of the upper floors of the building.

Many innovations in creating comfortable interiors are being tested today: automatic exterior shutters that respond to the interior temperature, building facades protected by a system of climbing plants (termed "living walls") that filter the unwanted intensity of the summer sun yet admit winter sun when the leaves

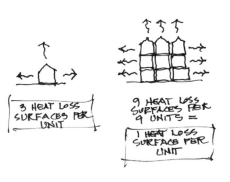

3 HEAT LOSS SURFACES PER UNIT

9 HEAT LOSS SURFACES FER 9 UNITS = 1 HEAT LOSS SURFACE PER UNIT

fall, and the use of the earth's constant temperature heat sink as a source for heating and cooling.

Our future holds the promise of more responsive, efficient, and sustainable temperature control. But we will certainly retain the deep-set pleasures of sitting around a live wood fire in cool weather or sitting in the shade of an overarching tree during the hot summer. There is an inherent pleasure in the contrasting temperatures, the heat of the fire on your face combined with the chill of the snow all around, or, alternatively, the cool of the grass in the shade combined with the heat of the day. This pleasurable experience of contrasting temperatures is memorably evoked by writer Herman Melville, whose character Ishmael enjoys a few nights in a warm bed before setting off in pursuit of Moby Dick:

> [If] . . . the tip of your nose or the crown of your head be slightly chilled, why then, indeed, in the general consciousness you feel most delightfully and unmistakably warm. For this reason a sleeping apartment should never be furnished with a fire, which is one of the luxurious discomforts of the rich. For the height of this sort of deliciousness is to have nothing but the blankets between you and your snugness and the cold of the outer air. Then there you lie like the one warm spark in the heart of an arctic crystal.[4]

As we become better at creating sustainable interior climates, we don't want to lose these more basic and raw thermal delights.

SAFETY FROM OUTSIDE THREATS

In Chapter 3 we described *firmitas* as the need for structures to resist and work with the forces of nature. This strength will protect the inhabitants from collapse during storms and earthquakes, but they further require safety from unwelcome intruders—animals wild and

---

[4] Herman Melville, *Moby Dick*, 1851, Chapter 11.

human. Of course, doors, windows, locks, and alarms need to be secure and dependable, but this is hardly an architectural problem. Nor is the prevention of violence by armed psychopaths or by terrorists. An architectural concern, however, is how to render our spaces less vulnerable to such intrusions at the same time that they welcome our guests.

One of the best approaches to creating safety seems to be to put as many "eyes" on the public spaces as possible, to increase the visibility of spaces by the users, neighbors, and passersby. Architect and educator Grant Hildebrand has explained how some security can be obtained via a pattern of space he calls "refuge and prospect."[5] Since time immemorial, humans have sought security in semi-enclosed spaces, somewhat shaded, and with an overlook to the brighter outdoors beyond and below. We can see this pattern in the raised terraces overlooking the sidewalk in Frank Lloyd Wright's Robie House, in the raised covered entries of some steps of museums and libraries, or

on a more modest scale in the outdoor tables up against a cafe wall, under a protective awning, with an overlook of all the pedestrian and vehicular traffic beyond. We may not be totally safe from assailants in these cases, but our position in space reinforces our feeling of safety: We have a solid back, and we can see them better than they can see us due to our shade and slight elevation.

The ideal "refuge and prospect" space embodies a smooth transition between the two

Refuge and prospect, after the Van Gogh painting "Cafe Terrace at Night" (1888).

[5] Discussed in his book *Origins of Architectural Pleasure*, University of California Press, 1999.

extremes, enabling the
inhabitants to locate
themselves at just the
right amount of protec-
tion versus exposure.

The archetypal "refuge and prospect" space in a home is the front
porch: One may retreat to the safety of the house interior, be more
daring and sit out on the front steps, or find the right position any-
where in between. The built porch is solid and unchanging, but the users can constantly change their use of it as appropriate to the weather,
their activities, and their moods.

Freestanding single-family homes can be made to feel (and be)
more secure by allowing neighbors to see each others' porches and
front doors. A kitchen window overlooking the entry helps you see
who is coming before they arrive. A low fence and gate before the front
yard declare ownership and potential overlook.

Residential outdoor spaces like courtyards are made safer by
having house entries facing these inner spaces, allowing views onto
them, and by communal amenities such as laundries, playgrounds,
vegetable gardens, and bike racks, as is common in European multi-
family housing.

Urban squares and plazas require dependable pedestrian traffic
through and past them, encouraged by ground-level shops and restaurants that remain open for most of the day and night, as well as generous opportunities for taking a rest and sitting to observe all the action.

BUILDING CODES FOR SAFETY AND HEALTH

In the previous chapter on *firmitas* we discussed the fact that a city's
adopted building code attempts to guarantee that a structure will be
strong enough to withstand the extremes of wind, rain, snow, and

earthquake without collapsing and harming the inhabitants. But the building code also tries to ensure the safety of more normal everyday use in several ways. If the structure isn't safe in this broader sense, it isn't really useful. If the inhabitants can't escape the building in case of fire or other danger, the building cannot be useful in the short run, and if they can't get fresh air or adequate sunlight, or must inhale fumes from noxious materials, the building isn't useful in the long run either.

To be useful to us in the long run, our environment must enable us to withstand the typical dangers that we subject ourselves to as we work, play, run, and sleep-walk through it. We inadvertently (and stupidly) cause many dangerous fires, for example, by smoking in bed, forgetting a frying pan on the stove, or trying to dispose of Christmas trees by burning them in the fireplace, all of which call for fire and smoke alarms and easy egress. We also need protection from thoughtless and potentially dangerous design: spaces with inadequate light and air, too few passageways and exits to prevent panic during emergency egress, missing barriers to prevent accidental falls, or poorly designed stairs that cause us to trip, fall, and injure ourselves. And we need protection from interior materials that, unbeknownst to us, may cause health problems, particularly if they were to catch fire and burn, releasing toxic chemicals in smoke.

We relish risk and danger when we choose it—we love to race, climb, and fly—but then we willingly take the responsibility for our resulting mishaps. We don't, however, accept unnecessary danger in the built environment, and our society's building codes attempt to ensure a reasonable amount of safety.

The U.S. building codes are relatively new, first written only around 100 years ago. They were originally developed as public health measures, a response to some terrible fires that led to extensive loss of life and to excessively crowded conditions in tenements with insufficient plumbing, sunlight, and fresh air. One of the most horrific events, the 1911 Triangle Shirtwaist Factory fire in New York City, took the lives of 146 garment workers who were unable to escape the burning building. As a result, labor unions successfully pressured for and won extensive new items of legislation that covered adequate egress and fire protection, and, in addition, stipulated standards for adequate sanitary facilities and maximum working hours.

Today, most cities across America adopt some version of the International Building Code (IBC), which covers a wide range of health issues for the users that improve the usefulness of a building. Examples include the size and arrangement standards for rooms, hallways, doors, and stairways; minimum standards for the fire resistance of materials and assemblies and for the frequency of drinking fountains, toilets, lavatories, and bathing facilities; and minimum amounts of window area for natural daylight.

The IBC not only protects the current users of a building but also the future users. Although an owner may wish to avoid some aspect of the code—because of cost, inconvenience, or aesthetic preference—and may feel that the code interferes with inherent property rights, the code protects all of us from danger. Adherence to the code is a price we pay for security. This price includes the additional cost for the required materials, spaces, and systems. Even in a private house, for instance, the materials must comply with tested safety standards and the spaces must have minimum height and floor space requirements. In some locales, a fire sprinkler system must be installed.

There are many such code requirements, and some of them may have potentially negative aesthetic effects. It may be challenging, for example, both to adhere to the code and to place the required electrical outlets, thermostats, and lighting fixtures in logical and harmonious locations, or to provide legal handrails on dramatically unusual stairways. And codes can also complicate efforts to remodel older structures that may have complied with earlier codes but no longer do. The building department will often demand that extensive remodeling of part of a non-compliant building must bring the entire building up to current codes. That requirement may make the conversion uneconomical, resulting in a total teardown and the need for a complete new building.

The building code sets *minimum* standards, which are not typically optimal from a usefulness standpoint. It is always possible to comply with a minimum specification, but to fall far short of optimal utility. A room's window may have the required minimum area but be located in a position that prevents a desirable view out, looks out onto an unpleasant scene, or blocks the entry of warming winter sunlight. The building codes succeed in preventing many dangerous situations, minimizing many health risks and setting minimum levels of usability, but they are not necessarily useful in the many other ways that are important to us: functionality for our activities, as well as physical and emotional comfort.

There is also the danger of thoughtlessly designing to simply satisfy the building code: using the minimum requirements, rather than what would be best for all the inhabitants. Instead of referring to the building as being "up to code," we might better say in such a case that it is "down to code." The advantages of building codes (there are many) and the disadvantages (there are several) notwithstanding, the realization of architecture depends on compliance with them. The most exciting and promising designs that can't receive a building permit will remain dreams and will not become architecture.

Adherence to the codes doesn't prevent the design of exciting spaces or adventurous behavior within them. One can still run, jump, and fly through them. The code doesn't prevent sliding down the banister, getting up on the roof through a hatch or a ladder, or leaping out from a window (first story only, please). If we want to flirt with a

feeling of more exposure, roofs can be habitable, the stairs and railings can be made of transparent material (as in the Dutch Embassy in

Berlin by Rem Koolhaas), or the railings can even be set below eye level (drawing facing page).

THE BUILDING CODES AND ACCESSIBILITY

For us to exist in, use, and move through our environment, it must respond to the physical capabilities of our bodies. We each have physical limits that change dramatically as we age. Typically, spaces and their components have been scaled to the abilities of a healthy adult, which has often left children and the elderly at a disadvantage. But this is changing—the activism of the disabled community has led to radically enhanced accessibility for the blind and wheelchair-bound. Gentle ramps, accompanying handrails, elevator access, door swings and hardware types, redesigned plumbing layouts, and hall widths have all been introduced into the building code to increase accessibility for those with physical limitations.

It is interesting that such modifications can render the environment more accessible for everyone, not just for those who absolutely depend on it. We all benefit from the availability of elevators, ramps (think walking with luggage on wheels), and generous bath and toilet facilities. Kids benefit from the lower drinking fountains (and urinals) needed by those in wheelchairs. Areas of lowered kitchen counters are useful for anyone kneading bread dough or other tasks involving downward pressure. Design based on this recognition is termed "Universal Design," and it promises to eliminate the stigmas and hardships associated with limited physical capacities.

The effort to increase accessibility can occasionally go too far. Our hometown of Berkeley is on the forefront of accessible design, first led by the pioneering Center for Independent Living. The

street intersections are all provided with sloping curb cuts that enable wheelchairs to smoothly negotiate the town. But this enthusiasm has extended to the steepest streets in the hills above the town. It is impossible for a wheelchair to negotiate these very steep streets, rendering the curb cuts useless. But in the larger picture, the town takes great justifiable pride in going beyond the code, having just opened a service campus for accessibility in the heart of town, closely linked with rapid transit, offering services for all with physical limitations.

Design for the disabled can occasionally, and comically, forget the abled. Glass protective barriers must contain holes for the passage of money and vocal interchange—yes, for those in wheelchairs, but what about everyone else?

Having made spaces ultimately useful through thermal comfort and physical safety, we turn to their broader uses. Next, we want our buildings to be functional by enabling our activities to be efficient and effective.

GETTING THINGS DONE: FUNCTIONALITY

A functional design is desirable in a house, important in a restaurant or store, and critical in a factory. *Utilitas* is the quality of everything functioning smoothly, efficiently, and economically. Consideration of the desired activities and functions of a place is where design normally begins. When an architect is asked to help with a new building project, the client usually presents a list of requested features, called a *program*, that must be included in the design. The program will typically specify the budget, a list of desired spaces and often their rough sizes, and a number of functional requirements that the client demands. After achieving a layout of these functions in response to this list of needs, the architect will also work to ensure that it is structurally sound and offers a pleasing and delightful experience. But get the functionality wrong, and the design will surely generate irritation and ongoing difficulties of operation for the clients who commissioned the project.

The program for the front end of a new restaurant, for example, might include the following requirements:

- adequate signage on the street facade to facilitate address and restaurant name recognition
- a waiting area just inside the entrance containing the maitre d' desk, seating for those customers who must wait for a table, and coat and umbrella storage
- a bar close to the entrance to allow customers to sit out their wait while having a drink
- a variety of seating areas offering a range of noise levels
- a variety of tables to fit singles, couples, small groups, and larger groups
- restrooms located toward the rear of the seating areas, with modest waiting areas outside the individual bathrooms, whose doors are not visible from the restaurant proper

These requirements, typical for most restaurants, will hopefully enable the management to welcome, seat, and serve the customers in an efficient, logical, and stress-free manner. Think for a moment, if these requirements were overlooked, how dysfunctional the front end of a restaurant might be: no visible address or restaurant name to help customers find the place, no indoor waiting area (only standing outdoors on the sidewalk), a bar at the back where waiting patrons have to walk through the restaurant to sit at the bar and wait, only one

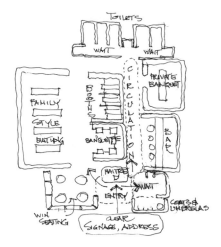

area for tables so that a single reading diner ends up next to a noisier family of six, only tables for two, restroom doors opening directly off the eating areas, and so on. Attention to functionality guarantees that a lot of awkwardness is avoided.

These various and typical programmatic requirements are often diagrammed: At left is a hypothetical diagram for the customer section of the restaurant.[6]

The program list of functional requirements is the most typical starting point of design, so it's important that it accurately reflect the needs and intended uses for the various spaces. Program leads to *diagram* of spatial relationships, which in turn leads to *floor plan*. In a good floor plan one can "read" how the people, products, and materials will move—how the building will "work."

This sounds deceptively straightforward: Gather all the requirements of uses and space sizes needed, diagram the interrelationships between them, and come up with a plan that incorporates the diagram. In reality, it isn't that simple. The list of requirements that a real design must satisfy is often very large and complex indeed. An effective program list must cover all the structural, physiological, psychological, and functional issues we have touched on above, as well as describe the relationships between them, plus more considerations that we haven't discussed yet. Not only is the list of requirements usually enormous, but the relationships between them are also quite complex. The hon-

---

[6] A diagram isn't yet a plan. It shows only the interconnections between the spaces, not their sizes or actual locations.

est architect will admit that a typical design is often based on a much smaller, prioritized subset of all the real requirements, or just those that seem to be the most important and interesting given the particular situation. A smaller, partial program, a honed-down version of the original, will permit a diagram and plan to emerge from it, whereas the larger, complete program might be overwhelming and simply impossible to accommodate in its entirety. An important skill that designers develop over time and after much trial and error is this ability to hone a set of programmatic needs to the essentials.

In earlier, indigenous societies, these functional requirements were fewer in number. This is partly because people's lives didn't change so quickly—the pace of new technologies and cultural change was slow enough that building forms had centuries to adapt. Each new building project could be based on existing spaces, those that solved most of the users' needs. Today, these indigenous, traditional forms don't work for our vastly more complex and demanding world, and we must design afresh, even knowing that we will be unable to satisfy all of our more complex needs in every project.[7] We must accept the fact that a new airport, hospital, or city hall will be shaped to satisfy many functional requirements but not all of them. As a result we must be prepared to adjust, repair, and remodel these spaces as our needs change over time and we discover their functional shortcomings.

Having touched on the design of spaces in order to ensure they will function well for their intended uses, let's shift our focus to our more psychological and emotional needs. We'll start with the basic desire for a place that one can call home, a place of one's own.

---

[7] The problem of gathering all the requirements of a contemporary design, organizing them into interacting clusters, and ordering them into a hierarchy of importance was tackled by Christopher Alexander in *Notes on the Synthesis of Form*, Harvard University Press, 1964. His opening sentence reads, "These notes are about the process of design: the process of inventing physical things which display new physical order, organization, form, in response to function." The key phrase is "in response to function," rather than in response to habit, custom, whim, or aesthetics. This theoretically inspiring but technically daunting method of design informed the later *A Pattern Language*, Christopher Alexander et al., Oxford University Press, 1977.

A PLACE OF ONE'S OWN

Have you ever had a dream of wandering through a strange city trying in vain to find your hotel room or home? Children sometimes actually experience this as they wander off and then try to retrace their steps. Most of us at one time or another have experienced the loss of our bearings in a city we are visiting. And sufferers of Alzheimer's often experience this disorientation, a fearful lack of ability to get home. Those of us who live in large apartment complexes can easily find ourselves on the wrong floor, unsure of where "our" place is. These experiences highlight the deep psychological importance of having a place that for the time being we call home, a place to return to. Architecture can help provide this by differentiation, by avoiding total uniformity, by creating a unique character for each group of habitations, and then giving each dwelling place some distinguishing feature such as door type, color, entry configuration, and so on.

Within the home, those of us in the developed world usually feel a need for "a room of our own," a private place where we can be with our own thoughts, dreams, and moods. Infants and kids up through the age of 7 or 8 often share a room, but at a certain point the desire for a private space grows, making it almost essential. This place will certainly be modified, decorated, and embellished to reflect the current interests and passions of the individual user. Occasionally a guest might be invited into the space, but only for a visit.

Because it is virtually certain that we will repeatedly move from place to place during our lifetime,[8] the next occupant will have to make that space newly his or her own. Can we identify any features of such a "room of one's own" that will render it ultimately useful for

[8] It is estimated that a person in the United States can expect to move 11.7 times in their lifetime.

almost anyone, regardless of age, sex, or profession? Here are some candidates for such desirable features:

- Natural light comes into the room from two sides
- There is a view that overlooks the greater world outside
- The room leads out to a covered private balcony or yard
- Circulation into the room and out to the balcony is straight along one edge of the room
- Furniture is not limited to one layout; there are options
- There is a spatial transition between the room and any public spaces

We suspect that a room such as this will serve a very wide range of users, from children and adolescents in families, to adults and elders whether single or in families, to city and country dwellers, to rich and poor. The 1977 book *A Pattern Language* contains many such clusters of essential features as these, called "patterns," individual parts of the environment that appear to be very generally useful, features that need to be there in order to fit basic human needs.[9]

A room like this may well be comfortable and pleasant, but that doesn't determine how it will be used. A full range of activities, emotions, and situations will occur in the room, some quite unanticipated. The architecture of the room cannot satisfy all the possible future users and uses—a bedroom, then an office, then a meditation space, then a music practice room, on and on. This is an example of the limitations of architecture. The architect's hope is that

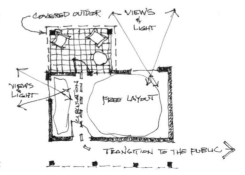

---

[9] Alexander et al., *A Pattern Language.*

by providing some essential features, along with the special requests of the client, the room will continue to serve future users' needs with only modest modifications and embellishments.

The architect typically brings these core features of a room to bear on any particular project, but also required is the ability to incorporate them successfully with the unique and particular wants of the client. A client's specific requests could include such items as the following:

- 11-foot-high ceilings
- a large closet for a collection of hats
- cork floors
- a window focusing on a certain tree
- a space for a piano
- wall space for a special painting

You'll notice how completely different such requests are from the list of "basic" room features above. Some client requests will be easy to incorporate, others not so. But one of the architect's most central challenges is to incorporate both the client's wishes and the foundational ideas that form the basis of his or her fundamental architectural knowledge. The client may not understand the importance of circulation in a room, but the architect must get that feature into the design at the same time that the higher ceiling height and piano space are included. And the synthesis must end up being graceful, efficient, and logical.

Thus, we build to satisfy two distinct but related goals: The space must embody the specific features requested by the client to support their unique needs and at the same time have certain basic features so that anyone else can happily occupy it at some point in the future. The first aspect means the room will have character and interest and the second guarantees that the space will work for many subsequent users.

PLACES TO BE TOGETHER

Complementary to our need for privacy is our periodic need for social contact, as part of a family, as part of a couple, or as a part of a social group with common interests. A couple needs a place to be just with each other, but in a family the children need to be able to go to their parents. Here is the beginning of an architectural problem. The most common solution is to create a distinct couple's realm, separate from another distinct children's realm, but with a clear path connecting them.[10]

A child not only needs a family but also access to peers. Playgrounds are ideal places for toddlers to play and socialize, but they need to get there and be accompanied by adults. Group housing with a central enclosed courtyard can provide such a space automatically—the enclosure prevents kids wandering off and the units' windows overlook the space for security. Even better, adults will be drawn into the courtyard if it includes shade trees and benches for relaxing, a garden that can be shared, and a common laundry, all features typical in European urban social housing of the 1920s and 1930s. Such a residential courtyard is an architectural feature that permits and encourages important socialization for the whole population of users.

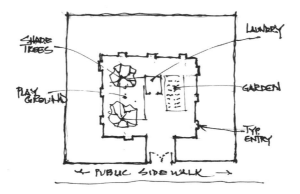

---

[10] For a fuller discussion, see *A Pattern Language*, pp. 645–655.

Older children, if they are fortunate, will be able to leave the house independently to find adventures and playmates within an ever-widening radius as they mature. If they are too young to drive, generous open space, bike lanes, and buses will permit them to explore the environment and meet others. In the city, wide sidewalks, narrower streets with overarching trees to slow vehicular traffic, lined with shop owners who have been around long enough to know the local kids, will all encourage safe use of the city.[11] In the suburbs, single-family homes can share a contiguous common backyard that contains paths, lawns, pools, playgrounds, gardens, and so on that serve a similar function of enabling people to meet others in a safe, more public space. Note that this kind of access applies equally to all of us regardless of age—Universal Design again.

As we mention children's need for adventure and socialization beyond the home, we recognize its experimental nature, its unknown consequences—sometimes including transgressive, hostile, or even dangerous behavior. A lovely courtyard playground is fine, but kids (of all ages) will occasionally want to play Frisbee® in the street, pull mischievous tricks on a neighbor, deconstruct a machine, or create some other type of ruckus. One architectural response has been the adventure playground, provided with scrap wood, rope, and nails (ideally, junk of all kinds), along with real tools that can be used to build, or equally fun, take apart. The lesson again is that we must not expect to make a perfect fit between the environment and what we think people should naturally want and need. We will always fall short, because once in a while all of us need to play with sensible limits, to take risks, to transgress, to upset and reset, to take apart and rebuild.

---

[11] *A Pattern Language*, pp. 293-296.

IN-BETWEEN PLACES

Earlier we talked about how spaces can provide a thermal range, enabling us to find a comfortable temperature as the climate, our activities, and our moods change. In a deeply analogous way, we need gradients of environmental exposure that allow us to find as comfortable a level of social interaction as we choose.

Consider all the many parts of the environment that are "in-between" spaces, permitting one to withdraw a bit for privacy or to emerge a bit into the social scene:

OUTER, MORE PUBLIC	IN-BETWEEN CONNECTOR	INNER, MORE PRIVATE
street	sidewalk	front door to house
front porch	entry foyer	living room
dance floor	edge of dance floor	seating at the wall
party room	deep connecting doorway	kitchen

In general, spaces can help us in our social life by offering both a link to the larger, noisier, more active social scene, as well as a link back to the smaller, quieter, less active zone. At a dance party, for instance, we first check out the scene from the kitchen or the edge of the room, gradually move into the center of the action to join in, then withdraw again to the edges to catch our breath and get a drink. Alcoves, chairs at the edges, a kitchen open to the dance floor, all give us an opportunity to be in-between, to be more with the group or less as our moods change.

The absence of in-between places can put a strain on social interaction. The absence of a porch and an entry foyer at the front door, for instance, means that a visitor has no choice but to barge directly into the living room. There is no place outside to prepare yourself for meeting others and no place immediately inside for the host to greet you before accompanying you to the group inside.

At the city scale, the same concept applies. The sidewalk is in between the street and buildings; sitting on the library steps provides both an overview of the city life passing by and eventual access to the inner stacks; and sitting at a sidewalk cafe is in between the passing parade of pedestrians and the restaurant within.

CONTEMPLATIVE AND CEREMONIAL USEFULNESS

Occasionally in our lives we experience a need for places of ceremonial gathering or individual quiet contemplation. The buildings that have held the most significance for many cultures throughout history have been those that serve a ceremonial or religious function. The very form and spatial organization of these structures grows out of their uses for specific ceremonies and seasonal rituals, or for quiet meditative states of mind. Such spaces help to focus attention on a ceremonial gathering, marking a human rite of passage such as a christening, a wedding, or a funeral, or to memorialize an event or person. They might also possess qualities that encourage us to turn our attention inward to quietly explore the workings of our inner selves.

These spaces often share a number of qualities. They may emphasize a special presence of light and sound. The Chapel of the Chimes, a
mausoleum, in Oakland, California, designed by Julia Morgan (1928),
and Steven Holl's Chapel of St. Ignatius at Seattle University (1997)
are two examples of structures that wash interior spaces, meant for
quiet gathering and contemplation, with colored light filtered through
glass elements piercing the roof. The presence of water—both visual,
as in a reflecting pool, and aural, as with the splash and gurgle of
fountains—lends these spaces a tranquil quality. At the Chapel of
St. Ignatius the surface of a still pool ripples with the slightest breeze,
reflecting the sky colors. And the gentle reverberations of water
drops splashing into plant-ringed pools throughout the Chapel of the
Chimes fills its many interior courtyards with soft sound, causing one
to step lightly and to speak in hushed tones out of respect for the dead.

Such structures may well incorporate and guide our movement,
such as the symbolic passage through a gateway, as under a triumphal
arch, or the procession down a central aisle culminating at a raised
altar, as for a wedding. Thus, the shapes of these ceremonial structures
often grow out of the movements of the ceremonies themselves, and
not the other way around.

These special structures often relate directly to the cosmos, as do
the circle of giant stones at Stonehenge that serve to mark solstices and
other cosmological cycles, or in the orientation to the rising sun of the
temple of Athena (the Parthenon) on the Acropolis in Athens.

Mausoleums are another building type that serves to shelter the
remains of leaders or saints in perpetuity, marking their permanent
location and reminding us of their lives. A memorial building can
also physically involve the observer with ascents (like the steps up to
the Lincoln memorial), or descents, as at the tomb of Napoleon lying
under the great dome of Les Invalides in Paris, arranged so visitors
must look down to view it, causing them to bow their heads. And the
pyramids of Egypt and Central America serve both as funerary monuments and as geometric forms of cosmological significance.

Contemplative spaces are sometimes created by artists to give the viewer a certain experience of the environment or of one's own inner life. James Turrell's light installations and "Skyspaces" are excellent examples of meditative places whose main purpose is to focus the viewers' attention, often upward through a ceiling opening, to the pure depth of light and space beyond.

Such structures are often placed in the landscape in ways that reinforce their role as pilgrimage sites. Because they are not easily accessible, it requires an intentional effort on the part of the visitor to reach them. The Chapel of Notre Dame du Haut at Ronchamp in France (shown above), by Le Corbusier, is placed at the top of a small hill. As you follow the path up through the forest, you view the chapel perched above from many perspectives, and upon arriving continue on the path as it winds to the interior.

COOPERATION: PLANNING THE LARGER CONTEXT

We have discussed several ways spaces can be useful to the owner and the users, but what about the casual passersby, the immediate neighboring buildings, the surrounding district, and the city at large? A building's usefulness must also be considered in terms of its contributions to these larger elements of the environment. The fully useful building will fit in comfortably with its immediate neighbors, not overpowering or overshadowing them, while adding to the cumulative effect of the streetscape. Its "front" facade and sidewalk can contribute to the graciousness of the street by providing a shaded, recessed entry that anyone passing by can pause in for a moment, or street trees to offer shade, softness, and a buffer from the passing cars beyond. At a larger scale, a building's plaza can offer the citizens a public forum—think Rockefeller Center Plaza in New York City, for example, and the way it opens up a long, wide space in front of the tower that is lined with trees, fountains, and shops, a place to meet friends, eat lunch, do business, perhaps reminding its users that they are citizens of a generous and exciting city.

Every time a new building or open space is built, it affects the larger surrounding neighborhood, for better or worse. A new building will change the neighbors' views, sunlight, breeze, or ambient noise level, often for the worse. But appropriate new neighbors can bring more interest, street traffic, and economic vitality. How can we limit the potentially negative effects while encouraging changes that are appropriate and beneficial?

The first answer has been through zoning, a city's planning code that specifies what type of facilities can be placed on a property and what spatial envelopes these new structures must lie within. An owner of a vacant lot or of an existing building who wishes to use these assets to create a new facility is limited by the zoning that covers that site, a code of permitted uses and sizes developed and governed by the city's planning department. Zoning specifies what uses that property may be put to, the portion of the lot that the building may cover, the parking spaces that must be provided on site, the height of the building, possible setbacks of upper stories, and so forth. If this were not complicated enough, the city is sometimes willing to modify some of these restrictions if the owner provides aspects of the building that the city wants: inclusion of a number of affordable housing units or of a community service center in exchange for an additional story of height, for example. And in some cities, neighbors who object to proposed projects have the right to ask for arbitration sessions, which the city hopes will result in compromise. In some cases this arbitration creates large delays, or worse, lawsuits brought by the unhappy neighbors against the planning department itself. Although this difficult and unpleasant process is rare, what is always true is that if a project is to go forward it must eventually succeed in getting a planning permit.

Zoning protects residential areas from inappropriate industry and commerce. By restricting uses of certain areas to commercial use, zoning can create intense, exciting shopping areas, and by creating industrial zones it can cluster the noise and commotion of factory production, keeping them away from quieter and gentler uses in the city. Zoning can also preserve sun access to low-density residential areas by limiting the building height of one's neighbors.

But rigid zoning can also create problems of sterility, monotony, and deadness. The financial district, densely packed with banks, brokerages, and associated offices but deprived of a more mixed composition including shops, restaurants, and residential towers, will quickly empty out at the end of the day and remain empty for the entire evening. Worse, it will remain empty for the whole weekend. On the other hand, residential neighborhoods lacking shops, bakeries, convenience stores, eateries, and civic facilities will similarly feel uniform and anemic, lacking any liveliness. To get to any services or entertainment, these residents must get into their cars and drive, drive, and drive. As Jane Jacobs long ago pointed out, the really stimulating and exciting neighborhoods will have a rather fine mixed grain of residences, shops of all kinds, and lots of people out on the streets walking to work, shop, and play. In short, she praised the life in a city that offered relatively high densities of well-mixed uses.[12]

Homeowners can sometimes fear mixed uses in their neighborhoods, worrying that traffic or noise will increase, or worse, that the presence of other uses will lower their property values. A recent local neighborhood brouhaha began when a resident with kids wanted permission to run a daycare facility out of her home for eight children. Although several of the neighbors welcomed the possibility, others were really upset. They were not only concerned about traffic, parking, and noise, but more concerned about how it might change the character of the neighborhood. As it turned out, the city was actively trying to incorporate childcare facilities into the residential neighborhoods and the proposal was completely within the local zoning ordinance. The facility went ahead with little disruption to the neighborhood. Many of the neighbors discovered that they genuinely welcomed the new life it introduced.

We have looked at how *utilitas*—the usefulness of architecture—includes physical protection and safety, the opportunities for both an inner life and a social life, and how it applies to how well our larger neighborhood and city work, that is, how well the built environment functions to satisfy our various needs. Before moving on to the issue of ecological utility, let's take a break and talk about how the role of function has changed over the years, how it went a bit astray, and how it is being brought back with a new urgency.

THE CHANGING ROLE OF FUNCTION

Throughout history architecture has embodied varying proportions of concern for *firmitas, utilitas,* and *venustas.* We may be over-

---

[12] Jane Jacobs, *The Death and Life of Great American Cities,* 1961.

romanticizing the past, but it seems that prehistoric and indigenous architectures kept them in balance with each other—certainly Vitruvius saw them as equally important. But during the Beaux Arts period of design in the 19th century, *venustas*, the beauty of the work, became the main emphasis, the most important measure of the quality of an architectural creation. *Venustas* was guaranteed by appropriate selection and manipulation of historic styles and motifs. A church called for the Gothic style, a concert hall for Baroque, and institutions for Renaissance. But toward the end of this period Eugène-Emmanuel Viollet-le-Duc, the architectural restorer, theoretician, and professor at the Ecole des Beaux Arts, re-emphasized a more rational design process based on explicit human needs and structural logic. His method was based not on historically accepted images and forms but rather on the programmatic needs and the frank use of new modern materials such as iron columns and trusses. In his *Histoire d'une maison* of 1873—translated into English as *How to Build a House*—he illustrates the design process by starting with the stated desires and needs of the client and combining these with his own notions of the functional requirements of any well-organized residence:

> The position of the kitchen is a matter presenting some difficulties. When you are not at table you don't like to have the smell of the viands, or hear the noise of those engaged in kitchen work. On the one hand, the kitchen ought not to be far from the dining room; on the other hand, it ought to be far enough from the chief rooms for its existence not to be suspected. Besides, the backyard, the outbuildings, the poultry yard, a small vegetable garden, washhouses, etc., ought to be near the kitchen.[13]

By focusing on the appropriateness of such functional relationships, Viollet-le-Duc brought *utilitas* back into the heart of the design process.

---

[13] Quoted from *The Architectural Theory of Viollet-le-Duc: Readings and Commentary*, edited by M. F. Hearn, MIT Press, 1990, p. 147.

At almost the same time that Viollet-le-Duc was teaching his students in Paris to design for desired functions, the Great Chicago Fire of 1871 destroyed the entire downtown area of that city, which was then gradually rebuilt with new, taller, more fireproof buildings. Among the architects involved in creating these new steel and glass buildings was Louis Sullivan. In 1896 he published an essay entitled "The Tall Office Building Artistically Considered," attempting to define how the design could follow not from a pastiche of styles, but from a rational consideration of the use and function of the parts of the building. The ground floor of a tall office building is given over to commercial stores, the upper floors to offices, and the top floor to mechanical functions—thus a tripartite composition emerges not so much based on aesthetic criteria, but on functional reasoning. He employed the functional forms of nature as an argument for his mantra:

> Whether it be the sweeping eagle in his flight or the open apple-blossom, the toiling work-horse, the blithe swan, the branching oak, the winding stream at its base, the drifting clouds, over all the coursing sun, form ever follows function, and this is the law. Where function does not change form does not change.[14]

His phrase "form ever follows function, and this is the law" has come to be abbreviated as "form follows function," a battle cry for many voices of the modern movement at the turn of the century. It is a powerful and seductively simple phrase, yet one can ask whether it refers to the form of a building following structural functions (the form of the first ground-level floor will respond to its structural role and function in supporting the building above) or the form following the human functions that are to take place within and around the building (the form of the ground-level floor will respond to pedestrians' need to window shop and find a lunch spot). Ideally, both needs

---

[14] Louis H. Sullivan, "The Tall Office Building Artistically Considered," *Lippincott's Magazine*, March 1896.

179

Wainwright Building, Chicago, Adler and Sullivan, 1891.

will be satisfied simultaneously. In the Wainwright Building of 1891 in St. Louis, Missouri, Sullivan and his partner Dankmar Adler expressed the three separate functions—ground-level commercial, topped with identical offices, capped with a top floor of mechanical and storage functions.

Sullivan once said, "It could only benefit us if for a time we were to abandon ornament and concentrate entirely on the erection of buildings that are finely shaped and charming in their sobriety." He said this in spite of the fact that he was a master of vigorous, organic decoration, which he restricted to entries and cornices.

The 23-year-old Austrian architect Adolph Loos spent the years 1893 to 1896 in the United States and was deeply influenced by Sullivan's ideas and work, but felt they didn't go far enough. Back in Vienna in 1908, he argued that ornament was positively harmful. In his "Ornament and Crime" he raged against the attempts to discover a style for the modern time, arguing that pure functional production was style enough. For Loos, ornament in architecture was both anti-progressive and harmful, ensuring that the work would become dated and obsolete:

> The evolution of culture marches with the elimination of ornament from useful objects.[15]

---

[15] Translated from A. Loos, *Ornament und Verbrechen*, Innsbruck, 1908, reprint Vienna, 1930, p. 2.

Villa Moller, Vienna, A Loos, 1927.

We quote Loos today as saying "Ornament is a crime." This is relatively easy for us today to accept in the cases of tools, machines, and furniture, but more hesitantly in the case of architecture. Given our long human history of decorating buildings, this prescription sounds harsh and severe. He expressed this belief in his architectural work, which is in fact severe but also rather elegant in its ordered restraint. The bare planar wall surfaces leave only simple shapes and openings.

As urbanism grew with its new industries and forms of transportation, and as science opened up new technologies and sources of energy, there was an undeniable appeal to the notion that decoration didn't really belong on a modern building. The combination of "form follows function" and "ornament is a crime" suggested that architecture could become more like a rational science allowing the architect to say, "Give me the functional requirements and we will provide what is needed, but nothing more." This was indeed "modern."[16]

---

[16] Mies van der Rohe later embellished Loos's dictum with the infamous "less is more."

Gropius House, Dessau, Germany, 1925. Destroyed during
the war.

In 1919 Walter Gropius founded the Bauhaus school in Germany,
which, until its closing by the Nazis in 1933, was one of the most important centers of Modernist design training. Along with emphasis on
form following function and the absence of superfluous decoration,
the school introduced an emphasis on designs that could be efficiently
and economically produced by industry. These three elements—
functionalism, undecorated surfaces, and economy—became the basis
of what we now call Modernism. The residences that Gropius designed
for the faculty in Dessau are good examples of this spirit of design.
They were wonderful buildings, creating a community of people with
similar interests, each containing generous social spaces, patios and
decks, and studios permitting some work at home. The example shown
here is Gropius's own house in Dessau. It was destroyed in World War
II, but the other Masters' Houses have been restored and can be
visited today.

If this 90-year-old building design looks stylistically familiar to
us today, it is because the early functional Modernists unintentionally
created an aesthetic style that influenced the whole world and much of

America's architecture today. The main critique of Modernism is that it became merely a style, a "look," eventually losing its commitment to function, to serving the whole range of human needs.

A low point of Modernism in America occurred in 1954 when a 33-block megacity of 2,870 units of low-income housing was built in St. Louis. It was a Modernist design: Each of the 33 blocks was an identical 11-story building, structurally efficient, with small but adequate units. The units had huge picture windows, creating a "penthouse" feel. But it also had fatal functional flaws. First, the lack of variety and individuality between the 33 identical blocks was not only deadening and boring, but it also prevented any sense of specific place, of home, of a feeling of ownership. And this uniformity was carried further into the units themselves, each with identical expression on the exterior of the buildings.

The second functional flaw also had to do with anonymity: A typical stairway served hundreds of units, meaning that residents were always passing strangers along the circulation paths rather than a smaller group of neighbors they could get to know. Residents were thus not able to feel that the stairs and hallways were "theirs," spaces to be maintained and supervised by themselves. These anonymous circulation routes became convenient spaces for illicit and violent activity, and the entire complex began to feel unsafe. The complex was never fully rented—only 91 percent three years after opening, and downward from then on—and with less rental came less maintenance and less desirable housing. Eventually, occupancy dropped to 600 units and the complex began to fall apart. As we saw earlier (see p. 81), the entire complex was demolished by the city beginning in 1972.

We also mentioned earlier that Christopher Alexander had formulated a detailed method for gathering, organizing, and designing with all the necessary functional requirements (see footnote, p. 165). In the late 1960s and early 1970s he, along with his associates at the Center for Environmental Structure, transformed this design approach into one that focused more on the psychological needs of people. As such,

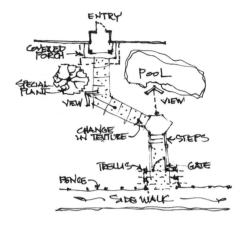

it was an argument against those examples of Modernist architecture that seemed to have lost touch with the feelings of users. The idea was that the parts of the built environment—the entry, the roof, the courtyard, and so on—could contain certain specific characteristics that would satisfy the users' psychological needs, and that if these characteristics were incorporated, anyone could go ahead and adapt it to the situation and site at hand.

For example, if the entry to a residence from the street to the front door incorporated some changes in the path's direction, walkway level, material texture, and so on, the person getting to the door would experience a change in mood, a preparation for leaving the street and entering the peace of the house. Such an entry was an example of a design "pattern" and was titled an "Entry Transition" (shown above). Once understood, this element could be designed in detail to fit the specifics of the individual home. In fact, it is such a clear and simple idea that its detailed design can be done by anyone, not just a professional designer. The book *A Pattern Language* contained 253 such patterns, ranging in scale from the layout of cities to the details of trim, and laymen as well as architects were encouraged to use it to the extent that it helped them design.

The book was quite controversial (and, full disclosure, Max was one of the coauthors). It was a success with the lay public, accessible to those who had no professional training. But many architects, especially those in academia, resented what felt like an incursion onto their specialized turf. They criticized its seeming bias toward Northern European

Vanna Venturi House, by Robert Venturi, 1964.

cultural values. And a few attacked its overall emphasis on physical and psychological comfort—comfort in the gardens, in the kitchen, on the balcony, in small shops, along winding roads, and in festival squares—resulting in a rose-colored vision quite out of touch with the real world of speed, action, excitement, and anxiety.

A competing notion of the function of psychological comfort was being touted at roughly the same time by Robert Venturi, then teaching at the University of Pennsylvania. He designed and built a house for his mother that similarly rejected the Modernist style of severe forms and plain surfaces, and instead revived symbolism, traditional images, and forms that harkened back to the past. The building reintroduced Michelangelo's broken pediments as well as traditional house forms like a gable roof, and surface decorations like a beltline and a broken circular arch over the door, all included for interest and fun (which we need too), but not functionally required in a narrow sense. These elements are not included to make the building function more efficiently, but rather to function as comforting allusions to "home," "roof," and "entry."

Venturi did not reject function—he spoke, after all, as a practicing architect—but he recognized that it must be broadened to include

185

our need for the familiar and remembered forms that still speak to us. The gable roof may not be strictly functional from a structural or usage standpoint, but it has an emotional power that says "home." And Venturi embraced the fact that we humans embody complexities and contradictions that cannot be ignored. As he wrote:

I am for messy vitality over obvious unity. . . . I am for richness of meaning rather than clarity of meaning; for the implicit function as well as the explicit function.[17]

Venturi, credited as one of the most important Postmodernists, will always be remembered for his retort to Mies, "Less is a bore."

Postmodernism is often ironic, as if the buildings had a wry smile on their facade, as illustrated by the 1984 AT&T Headquarters Building, now the Sony Tower, in Manhattan, by Philip Johnson and John Burgee (above). The building has a Modernist body but with a Classical base and pediment: It was a counterargument to the predominant Modernist style of urban high rises. The top of the building has no more function than to remind us of a conventional pitched roof, a classical pediment, or, as it came to be known, a Chippendale furniture decoration. It's irreverence toward Modernism, striking novelty, and sense of humor all combine to make the point that Modernism had merely become a style, sterile and cold, anti-nostalgic, and, yes, a bit of a bore.

---

[17] Quoted in R. Venturi, *Complexity and Contradiction in Architecture*, New York, Museum of Modern Art, 1966, pp. 22–23.

There is another even more extreme view of function current today among some architects. Put simply, it does not aim for psychological or physical comfort. It does not first ask that users have their needs met. It tacitly assumes that users sometimes don't really know what they need. Instead, the designs of these architects force users to stop and think, to wonder what is going on, to experience not just the complexity of life but also its unsettling ultimate unknowability. Their view of function is to make manifest humans' doubts, anxieties, and even loss of faith. These "deconstructivist" architects throw us off balance—they insist that we reconsider why we are here and what our purpose is. This is often what we ask of art today: provocation, not comfort.

American architect Peter Eisenman, for example, knows that his clients come to him not because of aesthetics, comfort, or familiarity:

They believe I will give them something that they may not be comfortable with in the present, but which may be good for them in the long run.[18]

The architect Thom Mayne, winner of the 2013 Gold Medal from the American Institute of Architects, describes architecture as "one of the most esoteric art forms of all the forms," and like Eisenman, wants to shake us up rather than comfort us: "I like provoking people. It's what you're supposed to do."[19] On p. 188 is his new building for the Cooper Union School of Engineering and Art in Manhattan.[20]

These "shockitects"—Eisenman, Mayne, Gehry, Hadid, Libeskind, and others—all want to shake up our thinking about architecture. They see their buildings as saying something important about society

---

[18] Quoted in *Architectural Review*, May 2013, p. 80.

[19] Quoted in *Architect*, January 2013, p. 27.

[20] 41 Cooper Square, Manhattan, home of the Cooper Union schools of Engineering and Art, by Thom Mayne, Morphosis, 2009. In addition to, or in spite of, the explosive and aggressive form of the metal screening surrounding the building, it is the first building in Manhattan to receive a Silver LEED rating, an impressive measure of the building's energy efficiency.

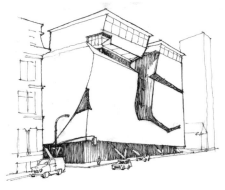

and the individual human condition, and it is up to us, critics, users, and observers, to sort out what meaning their spaces might have for us. This goes hand in hand with their view that architecture is an art, and like art, does not explain its meaning explicitly. Certainly these examples generate curiosity and wonder at the novel technical accomplishments, only made possible by advanced computer software and computer-guided manufacture. Their work has been embraced by the profession and by many powerful institutional clients, such as the museums and banks that want to create above all a unique and striking image. Evidently, this work is satisfying certain needs, bringing fascination and amazement to users, attention (and business) to the client, as well as fame and further work for the architects.

Of course, these striking buildings are functional in the sense of being safe and fulfilling their intended purposes, whether it be as museums, sports palaces, schools, or concert halls. What is clear, however, is that they do not express or celebrate their functions in any straightforward way. More typically, they express the complex formal ideas of the architect, armed with high-tech computer capabilities. In a sense, these are extraordinary works of art, but they are saddled with the architectural requirements for user safety and accessibility, for adequate light and air, for enough drinking fountains and restrooms.

Another group of architects and clients are primarily committed to saving the planet by building a more energy- and resource-conserving architecture. The acceleration of material and energy use worldwide leading to dangerous global warming has brought new functional demands to architecture. Our current buildings embody so many valuable resources, and then require so much additional energy to heat and cool them, that we need to transform how they are designed. Our buildings must start to incorporate a critical new list of (green) functional requirements if they are to help save the planet.

THE *UTILITAS* OF SUSTAINABILITY: CONSERVE, RE-USE, REMODEL

How useful is the built environment if global warming and damaged atmosphere, water, and soil productivity make it impossible for us to live here? If we poison our planet and are no longer able to survive on the earth, architecture will be quite irrelevant. What has become obvious to almost all of us is that we must radically alter how we build and how we live. In addition to all the other aspects of *utilitas*, perhaps the most important is that our built environment must help us to preserve the livability of the Earth.

Structures that waste energy through inefficient heating, ventilation, and lighting, that embody exorbitant amounts of energy in their material extraction, manufacture, and construction, may be useful to us in the short run, but collectively they ruin us in the long term. Unhealthy materials of construction can even ruin us in the short term.

For example, when energy is cheap, lots of mechanical air-conditioning and lighting makes it possible to operate a building, regardless of its design. As the price of energy rises, so does the cost of running the place, and attention turns toward energy conservation—better insulation, smarter window placement and shading, and more natural lighting. But when the price of energy starts to drop again, energy conservation seems, temporarily, less important. This was the pattern of energy price versus building design up to the 1990s. But a new recognition has dawned upon us, first sensed by our observation of new, severe weather patterns, melting of the ice caps, the loss of hardwood forests, the relentless increase in population, and a general degradation of the environment the world over. Scientists agree that our pumping of carbon dioxide into the atmosphere is the cause of an ongoing global warming that threatens the very life of the earth. In order for our habitation on the planet to continue—for us to be able to use the earth as a place to live—we must drastically cut our emission of organic fuel byproducts. Until we develop adequate renewable energy sources, we must lower our energy use.

Starting in the late 1970s the state of California began developing criteria for the energy efficiency of new buildings and introducing them into the building code. Other states have followed, and such standards are now an essential element of the codes that architects and builders must hew to in their new work. But this new vision of usefulness is not just codified into the building codes; other nongovernmental organizations have taken the lead in defining increasing levels of energy efficiency that developers and designers can aspire to. Institutional clients now routinely ask for levels of energy efficiency in their new buildings and boast of the accomplished results. Sustainability has become the new mantra.

From the standpoint of *utilitas* this is an essential new direction in architecture. As we run out of fossil fuel and as penalties for its use increase, the price of operating a conventional building will become prohibitive. From an economic point of view it will cease to be useful. By extension, if the inhabitants of the world don't adopt sustainable practices, eventually the world won't be useful for life at all.

The same applies to our water resources. Buildings can use immense amounts of water for sanitation, certain forms of manufacture and production (like beer), and landscape irrigation. Though cities continue to grow, their annual supply of rainfall is limited, and the utility companies must limit water use through increased pricing. Local building codes may also impose limits on water use, by restricting shower nozzle capacity, for example. Techniques for reducing fresh water consumption include the recycling of gray water (waste from sinks and clothes washers) for toilet flushing and irrigation, the collection and storing of rainwater in cisterns for later use in the dry season, and choice of plantings that require less irrigation (xeriscaping). In the longer term, returning rainwater to the surrounding landscape by reducing the amount of hardscaped impermeable surfaces, such as parking lots (instead of letting it run off into the stormwater drains) restores our aquifers, which preserves the availability of groundwater.

Although some current codes set minimum levels of resource conservation, a few architects and clients look far ahead to building designs that not only use fewer outside resources but also are capable of using none at all. Such buildings, currently designated as "net zero energy" structures, will be so energy-conserving that all energy needs will be met with passive solar gain, solar hot water heating, photovoltaic panels, and the internal heat generated by the lighting and by the body heat of the inhabitants. Such buildings will return all incident rainwater to the aquifer and will be able to purify blackwater effluent by the use of on-site biologically active ponds. In high-rise buildings, occasional floors may be given over to gardens for food production. This is the vision of buildings that serve us in an expanded and deeper fashion, not only providing sheltered space but also our basic resource needs in a sustainable manner.

We recognize today that a useful building doesn't tax the environment, unnecessarily using up valuable water, gas, and electrical supplies, preventing rainfall from recharging the groundwater supply, or heating with more gas or electricity than would be required if adequate insulation and insolation had been provided. A useful building doesn't leach poisonous chemicals into the ground. But we must accept that any new building incorporates a massive amount of embodied energy—in its manufactured materials such as steel and concrete as well as all the energy that it takes to transport and assemble them. So it is essential that the building have a long lifetime so that we get our money's worth out of those energy-rich materials and don't have to replace the building in a short time with another energy-rich building. A useful building in this sense will last, be repairable, and take a minimum of outside energy to maintain.

We currently live in a throw-away society. Our cars and appliances, toys and clothes are all built to last just as long as it takes for a newer model to be available. We repeatedly replace the old with new, wasting all the energy and material involved in fabrication. Before demolishing a building and replacing it with a new one, we need to consider fixing it up. There is too much new construction and too little repair, remodeling, and renovation.

This change of attitude is going to be difficult for many of us. Our society is addicted to the new, fresh, clean start. This is especially tough for those architects whose main goal is to build new. Yet there are benefits to preservation and remodeling that we shouldn't forget: Older places have the patina of age (not just the damage that can be repaired and the grit that can be cleaned), craftsmanship and quality of material that won't be duplicated, and the embodied memory of past living and design styles that constitute our history.

How can we explain the many cases in which a repurposed building is very successful in spite of the fact that the current functional needs are not part of the original design? Part of the answer lies in our affection for original materials that have taken on the patina of age. Another aspect is the nostalgic charm of older styles. And it is simply fun to be surprised by an unfamiliar and unexpected juxtaposition of a building type that used to house a quite different function.

But a deeper reason is that many older buildings have "good bones," basic architectural patterns that we find useful and satisfying. Evenly lit rooms with natural light, ceiling heights proportional to room size, honest expression of materials, and partly enclosed outdoor spaces are all examples.

As our society becomes more committed to sustainability, recycling and rehabilitation of existing structures will constitute an ever greater proportion of our design and building activity. Bottom line: We will need to build fewer new buildings and improve those we already have.

THE CONNECTION BETWEEN
UTILITAS AND *VENUSTAS*

A purely functional man-made object is often, as a result of its usefulness, beautiful. Loos was on the right track about this. It is easy to
come up with examples of strictly functional designs that we recognize
as being beautiful: some barns and factories, airplanes and motor-
cycles, tools and machines, cooking equipment and utensils. We are
talking here about designs in which the desire for beautiful form was
set aside in favor of a desire for effective performance. If you have a
cast-iron frying pan in the kitchen, it likely possesses this combination of total functionality and artlessness. The heavy iron spreads the
heat evenly throughout and retains the heat, resisting rapid changes in
temperature. The bottom is absolutely flat to sit firmly on the stove's
grate, and the handle incorporates a hole to permit the pan to be hung
above the stove, ready for use. When properly seasoned, it won't need
scrubbing after use, just rinsing with water; a wipe with a paper towel
and it won't rust.

If you agree that the skillet manifests a degree of beauty, you will
probably agree that it doesn't necessarily need the embellishment of
decoration to make it more beautiful. In fact, if the added elements are
inept, the effort will surely subtract something from its tough-minded
good looks. But the talented designer will recognize that as the developing object becomes more and more useful, as irrelevant aspects are
eliminated, a kind of purity starts to emerge that can guide expressive gestures, that not only
add to functionality but also
suggest, invite, and explain
usage. These expressions can
add to the object's beauty. For
example, the decorative embellishment of a building's entry
emerges from its function as

the recognizable place to enter (Where is the front door?) and as the unique entry that you are looking for (Is this the right place?); see the drawings above.

But does *utilitas* guarantee *venustas*? If a structure is functional, will it necessarily be beautiful? Most of the time, yes. But if its meaning, symbolism, or intent is abhorrent to us, our aesthetic pleasure will immediately melt away. Beauty, our focus in the next chapter, is complex, involving intellectual and emotional aspects as well as purely formal qualities. A prison is functional, but hardly beautiful. A bicycle assembled with a mismatched frame, wheels, seat, and handlebar may still be functional but seem awkward or inharmonious.

And can a building be beautiful and not functional? Yes, in spite of our view that they are strongly interrelated. After a building loses its original functionality for any number of reasons, we may still admire it. We can appreciate a building's beauty in spite of its uselessness—its inability to keep us safe, to enable us to accomplish a task, or to be economically viable. It may have become useless, but it is still dear to us. Berlin has many old abandoned but still attractive factories, breweries, and townhouses, but there is insufficient population and money to take charge of them to create new uses. And so they are often torn down and replaced with more immediately usable open green space.

We are left with the following situation: Although *utilitas* is an essential ingredient in the design of a new building, its resultant charm and beauty will most likely outlive its usefulness. It will endure, waiting, as it were, for a new use that can happily fit into it. We are touching here on a fundamental truth about all man-made objects, namely that what we find beautiful and delightful is at heart something that is both durable and supremely functional, even if we do not want to use it as intended. How else can we account for our aesthetic admiration for a well-built and functional object such as a tool, violin, bridge, or building? *Firmitas, utilitas,* and *venustas* each define distinct areas of architectural quality, but are at the same time quite interdependent, as these examples illustrate. Thus our perception of beauty is often linked both to the object's durable construction and to the fact that it was created from the outset to fulfill someone's deeply felt and understood requirements. ☐

"Architecture begins where engineering ends."

—WALTER GROPIUS

"Architecture is the reaching out for the truth."

—LOUIS KAHN

"I strive for an architecture from which nothing can be taken away."

—HELMUT JAHN

"When we contemplate the beautiful we feel that the object has a 'purposive' aspect . . . as if it were specifically constructed for our contemplation, and we sense a resonant or harmonious relation between the object and our unspoken sense of things."

—EDWARD ROTHSTEIN,

EMBLEMS OF THE MIND: THE INNER LIFE OF MUSIC AND MATHEMATICS, 1995

CHAPTER FIVE

VENUSTAS:
The Beauty of Architecture

TO RECAP, THE TERMS HENRY WOTTON COINED in 1624 for the three essential architectural qualities of *firmitas, utilitas,* and *venustas* were "firmness, commodity, and delight." This triad has become perhaps the most quoted version today, in spite of the fact that "delight" does not adequately capture Vitruvius's meaning. One problem with the term delight is that it isn't a quality of the architecture itself, but rather a mental response to the building we might have. There have been at least five translations of Vitruvius since then, the latest of which translates *venustas* as "attractiveness."[1] When we look up the definition of *venustas* today, we find "attractiveness," "charm," "grace," "elegance," and "beauty," all of which logically derive from the root of the word, Venus. Perhaps Wotton should have simply used the word "beauty" instead of "delight."

There is a further problem with Wotton's "delight," which is that not everyone is always delighted by *venustas*. In the face of great beauty, there are many other possible reactions: We may be intrigued (as with the Disney Symphony Hall in Los Angeles, by Frank Gehry), inspired (the Lincoln Memorial), awed (the Taj Mahal), or even

---

[1] Since Wotton, Newton (1771), Gwilt (1826), Morgan (1914), Granger (1931), and Rowland (1999).

frightened (as when ascending inside the Eiffel tower). Delight seems simply too frothy a word.

Vitruvius himself attempted to flesh out what he meant by *venustas*, the source of beauty in structures. He talks about two qualities that have the capacity to produce it. The first is *eurythmy*, which can be translated as "good shape" or "shapeliness." It refers to the proportion between width and height of the various elements of the building. Just as an attractive proportion exists between an individual person's width and height, there is an appropriate relationship between a column's width and height. The columns of a strong, "masculine" building would have a greater width for their height than those for a more delicate, "feminine" building.

The second quality that Vitruvius stresses is *symmetria*, which is not the same as our word symmetry (the balance left and right around a vertical axis), but rather refers to the relationship between the shape and size of all the building's components, to the proportions between them. Just as our fingers are in proportion to our hands and our hands are in proportion to our arms, *symmetria* is dimensional proportion between all the elements of the building to one another and to the building as a whole. These proportions can be prescribed mathematically. In the sketch below, for instance, each unit has the proportion of 2 to 1, from the smallest, through the intermediate, to the largest whole.

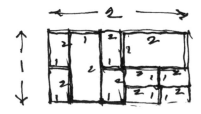

These are sophisticated concepts that remain valid and useful today. They didn't originate with Vitruvius: The idea that beauty emerges from proportion and geometric order was first expressed several centuries earlier by Socrates:

> If measure and symmetry are absent from any composition in any degree, ruin awaits both the ingredients and the composition.

This in turn was restated in Aristotle's prescription for beauty as "order, symmetry, and precision," whereas Aquinas later added "wholeness and harmony."

VENUSTAS AS BEAUTY IN ALL ITS FORMS

Throughout history, philosophers, aestheticians, scientists, and artists have attempted to understand and define the nature of beauty. The search is not over—indeed, perhaps it never will be. As a civilization matures, its aesthetic framework changes, expands, and develops. The transition from Gothic to Renaissance, and from Modernism to Postmodernism, involved a dramatic transformation of the notion of appropriate architectural beauty. But a maturation of aesthetic sensibility does not erase our appreciation of past works. Immersed in the built environment of our age and time we nevertheless retain our respect and admiration for the architecture of past ages. We respond to the beauty of indigenous architecture, of ancient monuments, of medieval cities, of all the periods of honest and earnest architecture. Architects often draw upon these past periods for inspiration and insight, and this is not necessarily mere nostalgia. As a culture we have an inherited aesthetic response to the heroism of ancient stonework, the structural genius of Gothic vaulting, the rationalism of industrial facilities, and the high-minded generosity of public works. Thus, we seek a broad concept of *venustas* that can explain the rich and varied forms of pleasure that we can obtain from architecture.

New York Public Library.

In this chapter we use the term *venustas* to account for qualities of a building that may generate a whole range of aesthetic responses, from pure delight, through strong interest, to a satisfying recognition of its inner coherence and unity. The aesthetic response can range from having pleasurable fun, through being tantalized by new stimulation, to a profound sense of the inner "rightness" and significance of the structure. We may even derive aesthetic pleasure from the recognition of the earnestness and high moral aim of the architecture. There are examples of structures that effectively combine these many aspects of beauty: the Hoover Dam, the New York Public Library, Old Faithful Inn at Yosemite. All are magnificent structures that we recognize as being well ordered, full of the complexity that stimulates interest, endowed with noble purpose in mind, and, to top it off, simply delightful to visit.

It is important to remember that we don't just look at buildings, though it is true in our culture that we tend to favor the visual, often to the detriment of our other vital sensory abilities. When experiencing built spaces, all of our senses participate; our whole body reacts to the place whether we are conscious of it or not. Our muscles and inner sense of balance are as active as our visual sense as we move through a place, open a door, ascend a flight of stairs, or rest against a wall. We feel the environment through our skin, sensing temperature and texture. Our sense of smell is activated by the materials of construction, the furnishings, and all the habits of the inhabitants. We even "hear" the building as an echo of our voices, the transmission of sound from the adjacent spaces and from the outside environment, each of which is affected by the building's arrangement and materials of construction. Here we want to include all the possible sensual impressions that buildings can offer in our notion of *venustas*: the warmth of a sunny seat, the coolness of a courtyard fountain, the smooth texture of a handrail, the aroma of rich wood and native stone.

Finally, we want to include the building's influence on our emotions and thoughts as an important part of our aesthetic response. Of course, we bring our prior emotions and moods along with us as we move through the environment, and they all affect our sense of beauty. The world looks good when we are happy, grim when we are depressed. But more important, we want to explore how the building itself influences our feelings and thoughts, inner reactions that can play a powerful role in our esthetic response. What we come to understand about the building influences our attitudes toward it. For example, we may respond to its history and purpose differently: Some love Monticello for its history as Jefferson's home and garden, others feel the moral stain of its construction and maintenance by slaves, while yet others are able to hold both feelings at the same time. But a sense of moral "goodness" often enters into our judgments of beauty. Plato rested his notion of beauty not only on utility but equally on moral goodness:

The beautiful consists in utility and the power to produce some good.

The beautiful and the true are often linked. Buildings may embody ancient geometric truths, incorporating the seeming magic of perfect shapes and volumes, the intellectual recognition of which can give us esthetic pleasure. The Golden Ratio, the perfect sphere, or the perfect catenary curve all have the capacity to stir our deepest intuitions and recognitions of mathematical order and sense of beauty.

And part of the "trueness" of a building (or sonata, sculpture, or painting) lies in its succinctness and economy. Both Michelangelo and Emerson stressed the absence of superfluity, of the un-necessary, in beauty. Michelangelo called beauty "the purgation of the superfluous," whereas Emerson put it this way:

> Beauty rests on necessities. The line of beauty is the result of perfect economy . . . . We ascribe to beauty that which is simple, which has no superfluous parts, which exactly answers its end.[2]

This is what we alluded to in the previous chapter: Pure functionality often leads directly to aesthetic quality.

Yes, the concept of *venustas*, of beauty, is complex. Think how complex our enjoyment of a beautiful meal can be: It involves the look of the food items, their aroma and taste, the interactions between them, their arrangement on the plate, our physical comfort in the room and at the table, the purpose and meaning of the occasion. Neither the cook nor the architect can control our initial mood and mindset, but both can orchestrate an experience that transports us to a fresh and beautiful place.

In the rest of this chapter we will look at each of the various sensory paths by which we take in our experience of the environment, starting with the power of visual perception. It will be a tour through the many ways in which the physical environment can help create an aesthetic experience as we travel through it, live and work in it, and pause to simply enjoy our good fortune in being where we are.

VISUAL DELIGHT: HOW DOES THE BUILDING LOOK?

What aspects of the appearance of a building are potential sources of pleasure and delight? As we know, there are wide differences of opinion regarding the relative goodness of buildings. But in the area

---

[2] From "Beauty," an essay in the collection *The Conduct of Life*, 1860.

of basic visual perception, there are some principles that can be stated and generalized. Some visual arrangements and fields simply possess a stronger aesthetic potential than others.

ORDER AND VARIETY

A balance between order and variety is one of the most important keys to an interesting and pleasurable visual experience. If the visual field is totally random and disordered, we only receive "noise"; we feel we can't engage it because nothing emerges as a form or an object. This is as true of hearing as of visual perception. In contrast, if the visual field is totally ordered, frozen into a repetitive, elemental form, we grasp its basic pattern or form instantly but soon lose interest in it. Our brain tends to say, "I've got it—so what?"

Compare the two very different arrangements of dots in the drawings below. On the left, the dots are arranged perfectly on a square grid. Once you see that and you get the underlying pattern, there isn't much else to say about it. On the right, the dots are randomly arrayed, without any order at all. On one hand, you can see the orderly square grid form immediately; on the other, the dots are so disordered that there is no form to perceive.[3]

[3] There is a relationship between the amount of order in an object and the amount of information that it embodies: Total order, where every aspect of the form is immediately known, contains very little information. We could call someone on the phone and describe the ordered arrangement as "135 dots on a 9 by 15 square grid," and it could be duplicated at the other end of the line immediately. And it's not very interesting, because there's nothing else to say about it. On the other hand, it would take lots of information to specify the position of each of the dots in the random array, and it would take us a very long time to duplicate it, slavishly going item by item.

Because there is no inner organization to the random array, there is no pattern for us to recognize, nothing for us to get interested in. It turns out that our visual interest isn't captured by either extreme of the order/variety spectrum. One extreme is too simple, the other is too complex.

You can surely recall a building that isn't visually pleasing because it is too rigidly ordered (or perhaps just a blank box in form), as well as another one that isn't attractive because it is too complex and confusing. In 2008, Minnesota Public Radio asked listeners to send in nominees for the "worst" architecture in town, implying the most unattractive visually. Not surprisingly, the responses lay at each extreme of the order/variety scale. A typical submission on the excessively ordered end, the Minnesota State Transportation Building, is shown below, where the facade is a perfect rectangular grid of windows, with no variation of any kind. Compare this with another frequent nominee, the Weisman Art Museum by Frank Gehry, visually an extremely complex, endlessly varying collection of forms (facing page).

This necessary balance has been neatly summarized by Stanley Abercrombie: "Architecture . . . must lie somewhere between total order and disorder, between homogeneity and chaos."[4]

Minnesota State Transportation Building.

---

[4] From *Architecture as Art*, Harper & Row, 1984, p. 149.

Weisman Art Museum.

CREATING VISUAL INTEREST: DOTS AND DABS

Thus we tend to take visual interest in forms that are intermediate on the order/variety spectrum. If we notice that order is disrupted somewhere, we become curious as to the source of the anomaly. And when we see that disorder contains a bit of order, we similarly become interested in ferreting out the source of that order. Take, for example, the orderly array of dots shown below, where the pattern is disrupted by some counterforce, or secondary order.

Our attention turns to the disruption of the simpler order as we try to decipher its source. In this case it appears that the perfect grid has developed a depression (or alternatively, a billowing up toward us) in its center, as if the grid was a rubber membrane supporting a heavy oblong object in its center. Visually the disruption creates a new, more complex form that holds our attention. In this case the disruption is not random but rather follows a simple rule for moving dots on either side of the center up toward

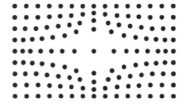

205

the edges. So in this case we have two different sets of order interacting with one another. The shifting of attention from one organization to the other causes a kind of reverberation that is pleasurable. It stimulates the eye and mind. It involves active visualization, real work on our part, an enticement to sort out the organizations.

In the example above our perception began with a hypothesis, a guess about what we might be seeing, a hunch that could bring meaning to the array. We want to see a recognizable form, and try to. As David Brooks has said, "Our perceptions are fantasies we construct that correlate with reality."[5]

This play between order and variety is at the heart of our perception of the world around us and is especially recognizable in our appreciation of music and the visual arts. In the area of graphic arts, for example, the balance between order and variety is what interests us in this 1983 screen print by Anni Albers (an early student at the Bauhaus in Weimar, and later the wife of Josef Albers). She titled it "Triangulated Intaglio." At first the print seems to be a totally free arrangement of particles, a bit like a snow flurry. But the more we look at it, the more order we discover: For example, the design is based on an underlying (but invisible) square grid, and each triangle fills one half of a cell within that grid. The variety comes from the orientation and frequency of the triangles.

Humans have been making patterns like these for thousands of years, decorating their bodies, utensils, and homes. The loincloths made by the Mbuti women of the Ituri rainforest in Zaire are extraordinarily beautiful in their designs, some based on simple arrays of dots. Our eyes move back and forth, exploring the variety, and are then pulled back by the security of the simple orderliness. In the example at right we can see areas where the horizontal lines of dots remain roughly parallel and do not cross one another. At a vertical line of dots the pattern is largely interrupted: Some of the horizontal lines cross the

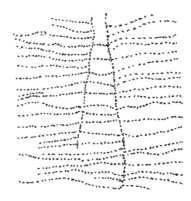

vertical border, others don't. A vertical border of dots is an opportunity for new horizontal lines to begin.[6]

We often use the term *disorder* to contrast the variable, whimsical, or accidental movements away from the basic repetitive drumbeat of order. But in the best works it includes a response to the pattern as it has developed up to that point. In Orissa, India, village women decorate the walls of their homes with elaborate painting incorporating semi-ordered patterns. The results are similarly beautiful to Albers's triangle design, but are due here to their balance between an ordered pattern and the spontaneity of its execution, done directly on the wall

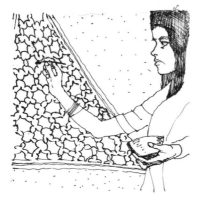

without a prior sketch.

Indigenous architecture— architecture without architects—invariably presents us with a dialogue between order and variety, between what the underlying rules call for and what is ultimately achieved in execution with the actual materials, ground, and builders. The excavated Neolithic site of

---

[6] Adapted from Plate I of Georges Meurant, *Mbuti Design*, Thames and Hudson, 1996.

207

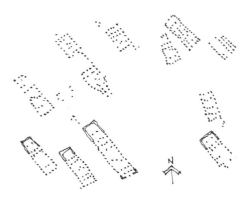

Sittard in what is now the Netherlands shows how large, long group houses were aligned similarly to the northwest and had the same orthogonal arrangement of post locations, forming aisles and bays and central open areas. Yet each house is a unique variation, responding to many specific local factors, such as number of inhabitants, the immediate contours of the underlying ground, and the skill of the builder.

Sittard site plan.

These examples of indigenous art and architecture have a visually pleasing balance between order and variety. Current design and construction practice, on the other hand, often lacks this balance. The modern process of design and building is no longer direct, with the creator imagining the design and executing it directly on the spot, using hand-held tools to accomplish it. Modern design is separated from the construction process by the need for drawings, by machines that build with little variation, and by the fact that others will build, not the designer. As a result of this separation, very little refreshing variety will occur unless the designer introduces it in the original plans, or unless the design itself responds to the small-scale factors of climate, locale, and details of function. The designer may introduce variety just for visual delight, as an antidote to the rigorous order demanded by the building culture and process.

CREATING VISUAL INTEREST: LINES

As a point moves, it traces out a line. Let us turn now to some of the visual properties of line, and how it can be used to give pleasure to our eye.

The line has given our eyes delight since humans started creating objects with pride and pleasure. Line is given to us by nature, with bamboo, reeds, and tree branches, all of which have been incorporated into utensils and structures. The Mbuti people who make such fascinating patterns of simple dots are equal masters of the seductive line, line that is perfectly simple yet mysteriously active and mobile. Are these movements in response to the creator's inadvertent hand tremors, or to the adjacent lines that have already been laid down, or to the shapes that are being created by the wandering lines? We don't know, but we can *feel*. We can visually redraw the design in our imagination and re-experience the instincts of the artist. And in the end, if the balance between the reassuring order and the mysterious variety is there we will find the work endlessly interesting and pleasurable.[7]

The qualities of the lines that are embodied in these designs include linearity (straightness), texture ("wigglyness"), boldness (darkness of color), thickness (width), frequency of spacing, and the extent

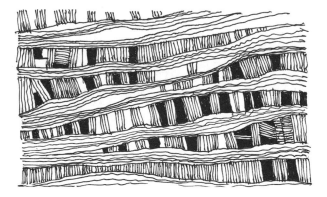

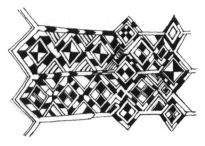

to which they are parallel. And lines can create areas between them, either monotonous or harmoniously shaped and varied.

This next patterned cloth, also from Zaire, integrates dots, lines, and areas into an all-encompassing visual field, filling the space such that every element has a clear form and is part of a larger design. At any point one chooses to focus, a whole and complete visual organization opens before one's gaze.[8]

These works provide wonderful examples of visual pleasure. It is as if the artists are playing a visual game, integrating a set of organizational rules with spontaneity and balancing order with variation.

LINES IN ARCHITECTURAL DESIGN

Architects draw lots of lines, each representing the direction, extent, dimension, and character of the various spaces and materials that will make up the building being designed. The qualities of these lines generate the qualities of the eventual building. Lines are used at all scales

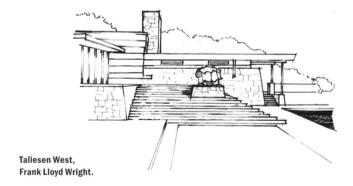

Taliesen West,
Frank Lloyd Wright.

[8] This analytical sketch is a portion of the cloth found in Georges Meurant, *Shoowa Design: African Textiles from the Kingdom of Kuba*, Thames and Hudson, 1986, p. 24.

of design, from city plans, to site plans, to building plans, down to the details of how the materials are assembled. An interesting drawing has a good chance of producing an interesting building.

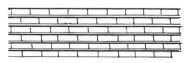

Frank Lloyd Wright loved straight, parallel lines, both drawing them and seeing them as part of his buildings, especially in contrast with the surrounding rolling landscape. His Taliesin West school and office in Phoenix, started in 1938, is a poetic statement of how perfectly straight lines can contrast with rocks and mountains and be reflected again in the perfectly flat surface of an adjacent pool of water.

In his Chicago Robie House of 1909, Wright had already stated most eloquently the power of the horizontal line in welding a building to the ground.[9] Creating the impression of longer bricks by emphasizing the horizontal joints between them while keeping the vertical joints tight, he thereby restated his theme of horizontality in the details of construction.

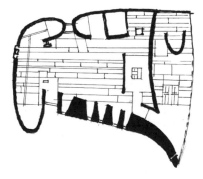

Le Corbusier's plan for the chapel at Ronchamp, France, illustrates a full use of line gestures, ranging from bold freely curving wall lines to a delicate grid-like paving pattern.

---

[9] The power of horizontality in a building design must stem from our need for horizontal surfaces for living, and for the calmness of the horizontal gesture as exemplified in the horizon and in the surface of water.

RHYTHM

Visual rhythm in architecture is similar to temporal rhythm in music: Often an underlying beat is established first, a steady, regular occurrence, equal in duration (called *tempo*), and equal in length in design and architecture (where it is termed a *grid*). This rhythm establishes the strict order, a kind of framework. Interest can then be generated by introducing variation: In music, every third or fourth beat might be emphasized, thereby creating *measures*—groups of beats that allow us to anticipate the next measure—and our foot happily starts to tap in sync with them. Each note in the music lasts for various lengths of beats: halves, quarters, or full beats. Our pleasure is deepened by our recognition of the measures, and how the notes can unpredictably fall between beats, or last throughout several. It isn't totally ordered, but it isn't totally random either—both order and surprise interact, giving us pleasure.

In graphics and architecture, the points and lines of the grid are slightly more complex than the tempo in music. Instead of being one-dimensional and following each other in time, there may be several grids: two for the horizontal plane (one for north–south, another for east–west) and a third for the vertical dimension. These grids need not be equal in their unit dimensions, nor need they be orthogonal (at right angles) to each other.

The architect or designer may now "play" with the grid by placing areas and volumes in varying ways into it, with halves or quarters, full units, or multiple units, just like the notes of music. Again, this is

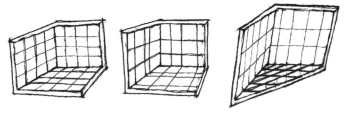

Space grids.

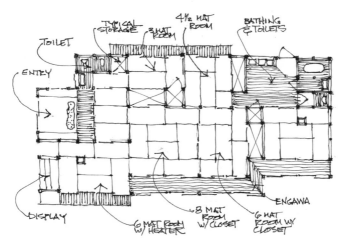

Traditional Japanese house plan.

where the rhythm is generated, where we see the underlying order and hopefully delight in the variety of the play.[10]

In Japan, traditional house builders based the floor plans on an orthogonal grid of around 3 feet by 3 feet. Working within this grid, each room was composed of a set of tatami mats, each a single modular sleeping mat of around 3 feet by 6 feet (very occasionally a 3-by-3 half mat was employed). The rooms were reached not by central hallways, but by a 3-foot-wide exterior walkway called an *engawa*.

Notice that each room has a simple rectangular shape, where the widths and lengths of the rooms are in integral number proportions to each other (3 units by 4, or 3 by 2). But beyond the pleasing shapes of the rooms (rough rectangles, not too skinny, not too fat), visual delight in the plan stems from the inventive rhythm between the mats oriented variously up and down in an almost unpredictable way, yet arranged both to follow the grid and to produce nicely shaped rooms.

---

[10] An interesting question is whether the architect begins with a grid and fits the function in, or whether the broader functional relationships and layout precede. The conventional wisdom is that design should proceed from soft to hard, from general, broad gestures to later discipline via a grid.

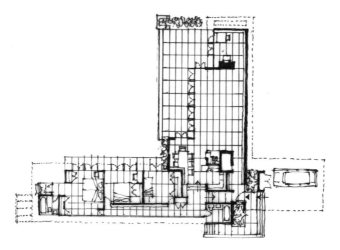

Rosenbaum House, Florence, Alabama, Frank Lloyd Wright, 1939.

Frank Lloyd Wright, a great admirer of Japanese painting and design, also used a rectangular grid for the floor plan of his Usonian house of 1939 for the Rosenbaum family in Florence, Alabama. This particular grid was also based on a modular rectangle, similar to the tatami mat in both its proportion and in its size, around 2 feet 6 inches by 5 feet. Almost every wall is laid down along one of the grid lines, and in a way that alone produces harmoniously shaped rooms. There is an additional level of delight in this plan: Not only do we simultaneously perceive the order of the grid (incised into the underlying concrete floor) and the varying sizes of the well-shaped rooms, but we also can enjoy the rare breaking of the grid rule. This is similar to syncopation in music, where we hear the temporary departure from the beat, which creates some tension, and its eventual reassuring return.

Le Corbusier used an underlying rectangular grid in his Villa Stein of 1927, where the unit width, like the traditional Japanese house, is similarly derived from the 3-foot width of a circulation path (labeled 0.5) and all of the other spaces are harmoniously shaped integral multiples of that dimension—either double, triple, or four times the unit 0.5. In this abstract drawing of the plan we can see the underlying grid

and how it is used to help organize the spaces. But Corbu has
another game for us to enjoy
in this plan: He permits a few
carefully placed curves within
the order of the plan, introducing another level of surprise
and interest. This is a bit like
a trombone's "slide" in jazz, a
smooth detour from the tone,
and a gradual return.

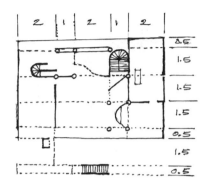

Villa Stein at Garches, Le Corbusier, 1927.

Rhythm isn't confined to floor plans, of course. Rhythm can also
be perceived in the façade: in the frequencies of the column spacing,
solids and voids, and window arrangements. As we indicated earlier in
the survey of "ugly" buildings in Minnesota, an incessant beat can be
unengaging, whereas a lack of underlying beat can be disorienting. A
balance between the two can create a pleasing visual appearance.

PROPORTION 1: THE GOLDEN MEAN

We touched on different aspects of proportion earlier in this chapter, but here we want to explore how proportion can lead to a kind of
"rightness"—and the pleasure we can obtain from looking at and using
a well-proportioned building. What are some of the qualities that lead
to this sense of "rightness"? Let's start with visual appearance and how
proportion affects our reactions to what we see.

We've used the phrase "harmoniously shaped," and now is the
time to explain exactly what that means. We'll explore this first in
terms of a simple rectangular shape and what creates a pleasing relationship between its height and width. If one side is vastly different
from the other we have a long skinny shape, more like a line than a
2-dimensional shape. If the height equals the width, we have a simple
square—simple but not really that interesting because we can see the

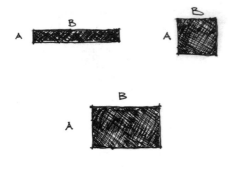

relationship between height and width very quickly and easily. There is no play between the two dimensions. But if the two dimensions can be somehow related to each other but clearly not equal, our eye becomes engaged, realizing they do in fact have a relationship to each other, one that merits further attention. A shape with good proportion, then, is one that we recognize as having a kind of inner relationship between its height and width, but one that may not be immediately obvious.

"Good" proportion between architectural elements is a major concern in design. For example, spaces for circulation (hallways, aisles, outdoor covered walkways) are normally long and slender in the floor plan, but the shape of rooms we inhabit normally need to be "chubby rectangles" or "potato shaped"—not too square, nor too long and slender. This is not only because of the interesting proportions, but also because a room works better functionally if it is a rectangle, capable of handling two social groups simultaneously yet still holding them together in a single space. Architecture is not only concerned with proportion in the plan view, but equally with the proportion between width and height of a space. As far as both hallways and rooms go, the height of the ceiling should be in proportion to the width of the space, with a wider floor dimension having a taller ceiling.

Although artists and architects may spend years developing a more refined sense of good proportion, we all have an innate capacity for sensing it, particularly when it comes to seeing "bad" or awkward proportions in the world around us. Just recall a poorly trimmed tree, a jacket whose sleeves are too long, a big building with an undersized front door (or look into the mirror and notice what elements of your appearance you might sometimes want to improve the proportions of).

These awkward proportions are usually due to the lack of a complementary relationship between the elements.

At the same time, the most visually interesting form is often one that deviates from perfection somewhat. The perfect cone-shaped fir tree will not be as beautiful to us as one that has grown in response to its environment, generating asymmetries, branches that are related to each other but not identical. And in the same way we are attracted to "character" in a person's appearance more than perfection, appreciating the subtle uniqueness more than the perfect standard. In these well-proportioned interesting cases we recognize that the elements are ordered and related to each other, we're just not immediately sure how. Our eye is energized, engaged, and pleasurably excited.

The proportion between the sides of the third rectangle shown on the facing page is more subtle than the first two. One can sense that there is a relationship between the sides but it isn't immediately obvious what it is. This rectangle is, in fact, a "golden rectangle," whose longest side is roughly 1.62 times as long as the shorter. A rectangle with this "golden ratio" between its height and width has the remarkable quality that when one removes the largest possible square from it the remainder is a smaller rectangle with the same golden 1:1.62 ratio. And you can repeat this removal of the largest possible square from the remnant again and again, without end, thereby creating an inward spiraling path.

The golden rectangle embodies within itself the seemingly magical quality of replicating itself over and over again as basic squares are removed from it. The pleasure our eye has in observing it lies in this *almost*

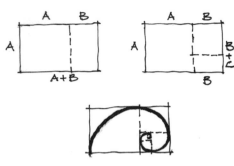

Golden rectangle.

217

apparent quality; we can sense the square in it and the replicated smaller golden rectangle that remains.[11]

Incidentally, the spiral that is created by connecting the diagonals of each successively smaller square is found repeatedly in nature—the growth form of the chambered nautilus shell and the arrangement of seeds in a pinecone, for example—which lends the golden rectangle an even deeper sense of "good proportion." As we grow up we get our first notion of beauty and good proportion from the nature that surrounds us. Because the growth forms of nature utilize the golden ratio, that proportion feels deeply right and proper in our eyes.

The golden rectangle has been applied not only to floor plans but also to the facades of buildings: the Parthenon on the Acropolis in Athens and Le Corbusier's 1939 proposed high-rise building in Algiers are two very different examples. The Parthenon's facade is contained within a golden rectangle, whereas the facade of Corbu's proposed Algiers building appears to be composed of three golden rectangles set one atop another. He then subdivides each section by removing a square area, leaving a smaller golden rectangle, which is again subdivided into many smaller golden rectangles. The golden mean is one of

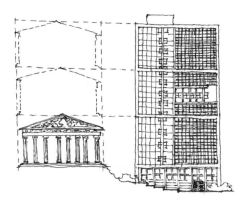

the many proportioning systems that architects and builders have used throughout history. Palladio, the great 16th-century master of well-shaped, interlocking spaces, allowed for several proportions of rooms, all between 1:1 and 1:2. Looking at the

---

[11] German experimental psychologist Gustav Fechner (1801–1887) presented subjects with a series of ten rectangles ranging from a square to one that was 5 times as tall as wide, asking "Which proportion is the most pleasing?" The golden rectangle was most often chosen as the most pleasing, and this result has been verified repeatedly.

EXPLORING
THE GOLDEN
TRIANGLE

EXPLORING THE
GOLDEN RECTANGLE

The golden rectangle is quite easy to construct geometrically, and once it is drawn it is equally easy to make an adjustable golden mean caliper you can use to measure drawings and photos to discover where the golden mean is employed. To make the golden rectangle, draw a square, bisect it, measure from the midpoint to an opposite corner, and lay that distance along the base to obtain the longer side.

You can make the caliper from stiff cardboard or wooden sticks: Take two sticks, #1 and #2, of the same length "C," and hinge them at their ends with a pin. Lay the ends along the long edge of your drawn golden rectangle. Place the tip of stick #3 on the square portion of the golden rectangle, lay it parallel to stick #2, and hinge it where it crosses stick #1. Make another hinge point on #2 to match the hinge point on #1, lay short stick #4 parallel to #1, and hinge it where it crosses. Here is the caliper showing the use of the golden mean on the facade of Notre Dame cathedral.[12]

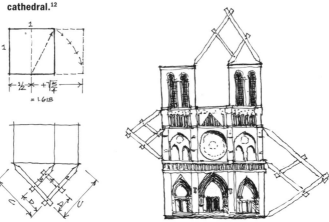

---

[12] The idea of building the golden mean caliper and using it to explore the proportions of Notre Dame and Corbu's high-rise designs came from Michael S. Schneider, *A Beginner's Guide to Constructing the Universe*, Harper Collins, 1994.

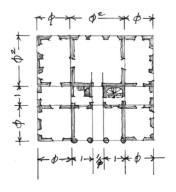

plan of his Villa Emo, it is interesting to explore the various ways in which he used an interlocking golden mean throughout his plan: the notation *phi* represents 1.62 times the unit 1, the golden ratio.

PROPORTION 2: THE HUMAN BODY AND THE MODULOR

Prior to the discovery of the golden mean, the earliest system of measurement and proportion was based on the human body—fingers, palms, feet, strides, arm lengths, and head heights. This system had two obvious advantages: You always had a measuring tape at hand, and a large person built a larger building for himself than a small one. Standard units of measurement were necessarily developed over time, certainly as a result of cooperation between builders working together on single projects. But a sense that there is something precious and beautiful in the proportions between these various body parts has endured throughout history. Certainly all traditional cultures have relied upon the human form to measure, using fingers, palms, forearms, and so on, and this has led to traditionally good proportions in their indigenous buildings.

An ancient source of thinking about good proportion between the parts of a building was also set forth by Vitruvius, who maintained that the proportions of architecture should be directly derived from the proportions of the human body. Starting with an idealized male body, the proportions of head, navel position, and arm and leg lengths to the man's overall height would define a set of numbers that could be used in the design of buildings. This was illustrated most influentially by Leonardo da Vinci in 1487 in his famous drawing of Vitruvian Man, inscribed in both a square and a circle.

Le Corbusier used a variety of proportioning strategies, but probably his most famous is his attempt to unify proportion obtained from the human body with the golden mean. In a sense he updated Leonardo's Vitruvian Man, linking the lengths of man's appendages with the golden mean, aiming for a formula that is used to 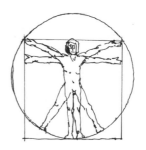 size architectural elements of chairs, countertops, door heights, and so on. He called this set of proportional relationships the Modulor, proposing that it be the basis for dimensioning in architecture.

Like most theories about architecture, both the golden mean and the Modulor are more valuable as guidelines than as rigid rules. Since Romanticism's emphasis on the individual, with individual physique, passions, and limitations, classically shaped formulas are recognized as inadequate to deal with actual projects and clients (whose size and proportions differ widely). Palladio used many different proportions, as did Le Corbusier. But as a guideline, as a rule of thumb, we can remember that good proportions result because they approximate golden rectangles. When Le Corbusier showed his Modulor to Albert Einstein during a visit to the United States, Einstein wrote to him, "It is a scale of proportions which makes the bad difficult and the good easy." This enduring sense of beauty in the various proportions between the parts of the body forms the basis of human measuring systems across many cultures.

ON HARMONY

ON HARMONY

This is a good time to mention the relationship between proportion and its cousin harmony. Harmony can be used in many ways; for instance, a song can be sung in harmony, with a second voice in harmonious relationship to the first. It is interesting to remember that stringed instruments such as the harp and piano create their notes with different lengths of strings, short ones yielding higher notes than long ones. During the Renaissance, much study was devoted to unifying the "science" of ideal proportion between linear dimensions of whole number fractions (1, ½, ⅓, ⅔, etc.) and harmonious sounds. (It would be interesting to construct a stringed instrument using Corbu's numerical series for the length of strings to see if they produced a harmonious set of acoustic notes.) In architecture, harmony typically refers to the relationship between elements of a building and its relationship with its surroundings. Harmony is also used to describe pleasing color relationships.

SCALE

Before leaving the topic of proportion in design, the word has other meanings that are important to mention. So far we have spoken about the shape of the building's elements, but we also need to focus on the size of the elements relative to each other. In spite of a window's proportional shape, it may be too large for the room, or too small, in which case we say it isn't "in proportion" to the room. We can say that a building is too large in proportion to its neighbors, or that the size of the trim in a room is too large in proportion to the size of the room. In all these cases, the item is "out of scale."

Yet as we discussed earlier in the section on order and variety, endlessly repeated "perfect" proportions among all the elements can lead to a kind of dullness, a perfection that lulls us into acceptance but doesn't grab our attention or interest. Architecture expresses feel-

ings and thoughts, and
scale is one of these
expressive tools. Frank
Lloyd Wright was fond
of making the ceilings
in his hallways lower
than one might expect,

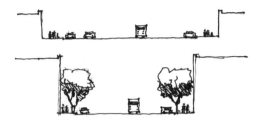

and narrower too, in order to contrast the passage with the arrival into
a room of a more generous proportion than expected. He is playing
with scale to affect us, almost to force us to pay attention to the size
and feeling of the room ahead. Exaggeration and emphasis of scale
between elements is a powerful tool of design, not just to be eccentric,
but to allow us to make "interesting deviations" from a scale we've become used to.

In terms of city planning, the width of a city street can be out of
scale in terms of the height of the buildings that face it and the pedestrian and vehicular traffic that travels up and down. In relatively
low-density areas, where the buildings are of one- to three-story height
and a street of 60-foot width can be too wide (encouraging high auto
speeds and preventing pedestrians from interacting with those on
the other side of the street), the street will feel out of scale with the
neighborhood. In contrast, in a neighborhood of six- to eight-story
buildings, like Greenwich Village in Manhattan, a narrower street
of 40-foot width lined with 30-foot-high trees will feel more in scale,
giving the street a room-like feeling, with more potential pedestrian
interaction. Note how the narrower street and the taller surrounding
building heights imply an outdoor room with better proportion in its
cross section, similar to a golden rectangle.

Then there's the other important sense of scale, not so much between elements of the building, but rather the building in relation to
us, to our bodies. If a room feels too small or too large it is usually our
body that is talking. Wright's low doorways are small in relation to the
larger rooms to come, and they also create a sense of compression in

our bodies as we pass through them, a sense that expands as we enter the room beyond. The size of a dining table can be out of scale in terms of our gathering together for meals and conversation, either placing us uncomfortably close to each other or too remote from one another to be able to talk comfortably with the person across from us. For a typical get-together, a table between 3 feet and 4 feet across works well.

In Le Corbusier's Modulor, the scale of steps, sitting heights, ledges to lean one's elbows on, and table and door heights are all determined by the dimensions of our bodies. Again, though, modifications from perfect scale can be used to make an architectural point: A higher mantelpiece over the fireplace, or a higher doorway, can emphasize the grandeur of a room, just as lower elements can speak of modest spaces, a more cottage-like atmosphere. These slight alterations from conventional scale can catch our attention and interest, hopefully leading to visual delight. The skillful manipulation of scale is one of the designer's most subtle yet powerful tools in capturing our visual attention. Above is the oversized fireplace Bernard Maybeck provided for his tiny studio/house, a gesture emphasizing the importance of the hearth in the home.[13] Out of proportion? Yes, but for an expressive purpose.

FIGURE/GROUND

Individual building shapes and volumes sit within a sea of surrounding space. Bring another element into proximity and they will begin to

---

[13] Drawing adapted from "Maybeck Made La Loma Park His Own Country," *Berkeley Daily Planet*, April 30, 2009, by Daniella Thompson.

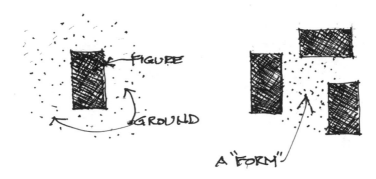

give a shape and volume to the space between them. The solid shape of the building's element is called the *figure*, whereas the surrounding space is called the *ground*. We don't tend to pay much attention to the ground when the figure stands alone, without neighbors. But when the ground starts to be surrounded by additional nearby figures something remarkable happens: At a certain point the ground takes on the apparent solidity and wholeness of a figure. From being a shapeless, empty, undefined space, it suddenly snaps into a form, something that we can almost grasp (perceive) with our eyes.

The architect develops strong figure/ground relationships throughout the design at all scales. Starting with a small-scale example, observe the following railing design (p. 226), creating as much interest in the spaces between the elements as in the elements themselves.

At a larger scale, building wings are made to wrap around and thereby give shape to whole, object-like outdoor spaces, spaces that as a result feel like outdoor

Some figure/ground relationships can be so compelling that once we "see" the form of the ground as a figure we can't stop seeing it, even if we try.

225

rooms. In the Moroccan town of Marrakesh the buildings wrap around and thereby shape private exterior courts. In the aerial view below left, the building roofs are white and the inner courts are black, but the figure/ground relationship is so strong that one can make the perceptual shift and visualize the dark areas as buildings and the white areas as the outdoors. In and out, solid and void, interlock strongly.[14]

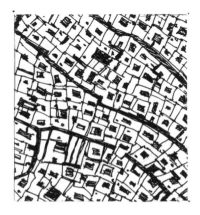

SYMMETRY AND BALANCE

Our eyes are bombarded with incoming data, and over time, from childhood on, we learn to sort it all out into meaningful perceptions. The existence of symmetry in a design or in a building cuts our perceptual work in half. Most living things embody some amount of symmetry, often bilateral symmetry, where the left side mirrors the right side. The axis that separates them is the balance line.

We perceive symmetry immediately and, to the extent that it provides a sense of balance and counterpoint to complexity, we find it visually satisfying. The balance and stability that accompany symmetry is especially welcome in architecture, where we need our buildings to embody just that structural quality: stability. Bilateral symmetry has

[14] Adapted from aerial view of Marrakesh from Bernard Rudofsky, *Architecture Without Architects*, Doubleday & Co., 1964, p. 54.

been a staple of architecture throughout history (the pyramids, Greek and Roman buildings, straight through the Gothic and Renaissance periods), so we should not be surprised to see bilateral symmetry in much of today's architecture.[15]

With the birth of Modernism at the end of the 19th century, architects began to emphasize a more asymmetrical sense of balance, often replacing the static bilateral form with a more dynamic balance. In this form of balance there is a center, but it is a center of balance that does not rely upon symmetry. Our bodies assume static balance when we stand ramrod straight, but dynamic balance when we dance, run, or play tennis.

This balanced asymmetry was present in earlier indigenous buildings, and modernism often drew on these indigenous forms, shifting to a dynamic balance in design because of a shift in the notion of what a building should be. Instead of a symmetrical facade being critical, it was now more important that the build-

---

[15] The artist Donald Judd wrote that all buildings should be symmetrical unless there was some functional reason for them to vary.

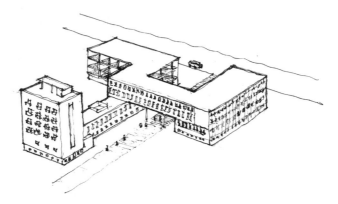

Bauhaus, Dessau, 1925.

ing be "functional," its layout in response to the needs of the program, the direction of incoming sunlight, and the differing available views. None of these things will produce a bilaterally symmetrical building. At around the same time, Japanese architecture with its more natural rambling plans began to strongly influence Western design, especially the early work of Frank Lloyd Wright.

So if a building is designed with all these varying inputs, what do we mean by "dynamic balance." What is it that our eyes see that leads us to perceive a kind of balance that isn't symmetrical? Let's look at the example of the Dessau Bauhaus, designed by Walter Gropius in 1925.

Gropius, the founder of the Bauhaus school, expressed the separate functions of the Dessau buildings and their relationships between each other. The teaching of painting, woodworking, and metal shop all had their unique requirements, as did the administrative offices. These functions were not symmetrical, yet there needed to be a center of the complex. As you look at the building complex, it falls into five easily identified sections. The two four-story laboratory buildings sit in front (on the right side of the above sketch), with a taller, almost detached student dormitory to the rear, which is connected to the labs with a lower auditorium wing, and a long, skinny bridge connecting the upper stories of the two labs and allowing vehicular and pedestrian traffic to flow under. If you had to select the center of gravity of this complex by locating the point at which to pick it up in a balanced way, where would you grasp it? If you answered the left-center of the bridge element, you're correct; it's the center of gravity, and also the exact location of the director's office, Herr Professor Gropius.

CLARITY OF FORM

Our eye seems to welcome the appearance of a building when we can see how it was put together, both in the large sense (how its major pieces fit one another) and in the detailed sense of its construction. Perhaps that is because we mentally deconstruct and reconstruct the major parts of the building as we explore and develop our understanding of it. A building that is simply a cube in shape does not offer this particular potential for pleasure, though it may be elegant. A building that is too disorderly will not offer pleasure either; it takes too much work to sort out its organizational rationale, and we give up. So a balance between a very simple order of organization and a more dynamic and vigorous arrangement is what will likely give us aesthetic pleasure.

The Bauhaus building is a good example of clarity of form: not too simple and not too complex. We can imagine taking the elements of the building apart and reassembling them, just like building blocks. Contrast that with the Viennese Rufer House by Adolf Loos, which doesn't offer this enjoyable possibility. There are no major elements of form brought together to create the whole. The form is no fun.

Rufer House, 1922.

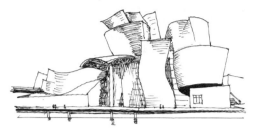

Guggenheim Museum Bilbao, 1997.

But Frank Gehry's Guggenheim Bilbao museum is an example of such complexity in organization that, although the building has many other visual pleasures to offer (such as a powerfully dramatic appearance with dynamic moving energy), clarity isn't one of them. It seems that the design is intended to baffle any attempt to describe how its elements are assembled; if it came apart, we wouldn't be able to put it together again.

Clarity is valued in architectural design, perhaps because it suggests that the architect has actually solved the knotty problem of satisfying a complex program in a simple, economic fashion. Architectural superstars like Gehry often forgo clarity in favor of surprise, uniqueness, excitement, or novelty.

HAPTIC DELIGHT: HOW DOES THE BUILDING FEEL?

What does a building feel like as we use it? This may at first seem a strange question, because we tend to think that buildings are to look at, not to touch. But we inhabit buildings as well as look at them. We lean against their walls, walk upon their floors, and may sit upon their ledges (like a *banco* in a traditional adobe). We open their doors, wake up in their rooms, adjust their windows, and infrequently bump into some part of them when we aren't looking. Without referring to the building's furniture (which we touch much more intimately), we look here at how we may derive some haptic pleasure (the pleasure of touch) and information from buildings.

There can certainly be haptic pleasure derived from the act of construction: the actual placing of smooth or rough stone, the smoothness or roughness of wood, or the plastering of a wall. Because most of us don't build the buildings we use, we forget this aspect of interaction. In 1973 Lloyd Kahn published the book *Shelter,* his collection of American hand-built houses, most of which were a part of the back-to-the-land movement. In 2004 he published his second collection, *Home Work*, illustrating more of the remarkable buildings that can be built by hand using readily available materials and continuing the tradition of indigenous architecture.[16]

Hand-built buildings are particularly satisfying to the sense of touch, as they typically use smoothly worn and gracefully bent wood pieces that beg to be touched, along with stones placed with a sense of where they will be needed for sitting and hand-plastered walls that invite a sympathetic re-creation of the motions that created them. Throughout history buildings have been shaped by handwork, and when we are in such a building our hands (and eyes) follow their work and find pleasure there.

Modern construction embodies far less handwork. But milled and sanded wood can feel luxuriously smooth to the hand; wood that has been planed with a Japanese draw blade can shine and glisten with smoothness, feeling even better. Extruded metal window frames are smooth and cool to the touch, and we can take pleasure in their preciseness. Wooden floors have never gone out of favor, and our feet appreciate the resilience and softness of them in contrast to concrete or stone floors; cork floors are even more relaxing to the feet. Sheetrock walls offer little haptic pleasure, but when they are smoothly finished with a thin layer of veneer plaster they take on a velvety surface that is irresistible to our hands.

Some architects are especially aware of the way our bodies interact with buildings. Alvar Aalto wrapped portions of the steel columns in

---

[16] *Shelter,* Shelter Publications, 1973; *Home Work: Handbuilt Shelter*, Shelter Publications, 2004.

his Villa Mairea with wood or rattan to make them more attractive to the hand. He understood that people would then feel invited to interact with them in a more direct way, leaning on and touching them.

There is a strong interaction between our senses, in this case between our eyes and our sense of touch. When we see something that looks attractive to touch, we can vicariously touch it and derive haptic pleasure, even though we are only looking at it. A good example of this interaction can be illustrated by the Wells Cathedral Chapter House, where the steps have been worn down since 1306 into liquid smoothness that we can feel simply by looking at them.

There is another sensual aspect of physical pleasure that can be obtained from architecture, and that has to do with how our bodies feel as we move through the building. As we climb stairs, or lean on a low wall, we not only feel the building on our skin but we also feel it in our muscles and joints. This inner body sense is called proprioception, the ability to sense the position, location, orientation, and movement of the body and its parts. A well-designed flight of stairs, with the proper relationship between the risers and the treads,[17] will be pleasurable to use: We will be able to adjust our pace, rhythm, arm swing, length of stride, and angle of forward-leaning to ascend or descend most gracefully and effortlessly.[18] Once a ratio between riser and tread has been established, it is essential that it be maintained throughout the entire flight of stairs. The cruelest misanthrope will design or build a flight

---

[17] The simplest relationship is the tread length plus the riser height should total around 17 inches to 18 inches.

[18] Effortlessness isn't always what we want in a building. The doors to a bank or courthouse should have heft, and we should feel the effort in climbing the steps up to the top of a tower in our legs.

of stairs where this ratio is varied somewhere unexpected along the flight, which will invariably cause an unpleasant proprioceptive jolt, or worse, a serious fall.

Our feet tell us a lot about where we are and what the appropriate behavior in that space should be, all because of the "feel" of the materials we are walking on. We leave the asphalt in the road, step up to concrete on the pedestrian sidewalk, slowly meander up a gravel path to a house, wipe our feet on a rubber door mat, step in to be greeted on the tiled entry, and are led across the wooden floor of the hallway to our seat in the carpeted living room. These varying floor feelings have a deep effect on our experience of spaces and how we are to use them.

Our inner body sense will also be very aware of any movements of the building itself: a strong wind or minor earthquake affecting a wood-frame building, or the slower, larger perturbations of a very tall building, again due to wind or earthquake. These motions can produce a pleasant reaction if you are in a tent or a tree house, where such motion can be expected, but they can be frightening (or nauseating) in a permanent building where we expect solidity at all times.

Similarly, a little bounciness in the floor can be pleasant if it is harmonious with the intended use of the room. A softer, more yielding floor can be very welcome in a workshop or kitchen where you are generally working on your feet. A dance floor or a gym floor should be just a little bouncy or springy to give a feeling of lightness to your step. Users of a building may feel queasy as an elevator slows or accelerates. And very high balconies can be alarming as you get closer to the edge.

The architect needs to keep the users in mind during design, asking how they will physically feel as they move through the eventual building. A totally rigid building may feel too hard, even severe, whereas an excessively flexible building may feel too insubstantial and fragile.[19] You can take pleasure in feeling a building respond modestly to the wind or an earthquake, knowing that these self-correcting

---

[19] This is not an unusual occurrence, especially in residential buildings, where a floor joist may be perfectly adequate structurally yet result in an excessively bouncy floor.

movements are part of the building's ability to withstand its environment over the long term. Like a tree that bends in the wind, it responds but does not snap in two.

ACOUSTIC DELIGHT: HOW DOES THE BUILDING SOUND?

Buildings make noises and shape the sounds we make as we use them. They may creak in the wind and transmit the sound of rain and hail falling on the roof, and their lights and heating devices may buzz or whir. As long as the building is performing well—keeping the rain out of the interior, for example—we are reassured and find such noises pleasurable. As it is said, "When the house is strong, the storm is good."

Heavy stone structures with thick sealed window and door openings keep outdoor noises out and can offer an unusual quietness inside. This quality can, by contrast, magnify noises produced internally, such as voices and slamming doors. And these heavy solid buildings often have hard interior materials—stone, brick, or plaster—causing interior noises to bounce endlessly within the structure and creating a sustained reverberation of sound, even echoes. This can give an unpleasant feeling of harshness or coldness, a clangy acoustic atmosphere where it can be difficult to hear conversation and the details of music. It gets a bit muddled. This is one of the reasons that tapestries and rugs are needed in castles—to dampen out the reverberation of sounds. Contemporary buildings with hard interior surfaces similarly require acoustic dampening to make them feel habitable. Just think of how differently a space "sounds" before moving in, before bringing in rugs, furniture, books, and all sorts of softer material.

Lighter wood-framed buildings transmit sounds from the exterior and from room to room and floor to floor. In such buildings we aren't surprised to hear footsteps from the room above or noise from the adjacent room. Indeed, this can be reassuring, helping inhabitants to be aware of each other's presence and movements.

A space intended for musical or theatrical performances is an interesting case where the designer will want the entire room to have a degree of resonance, acting a bit like an instrument itself, vibrating in sympathy with the music and voices, as a cello resonates and amplifies the vibrating strings.[20]

Restaurants have their own acoustic issues. A bright acoustic buzz in the dining room has come to indicate that the restaurant is a success, that lots of people are enjoying themselves, that you are not alone. Music is piped in to start the background noise, often an indistinguishable thudding bass drum beat that gets one to bob in rhythm, but with no real melody to grab one's attention. The music is augmented by lots of hard surfaces in the interior that bounce the sounds around, creating a general hubbub of "action." As more folks actually arrive, the noise builds because one needs to speak to one's companions louder just to be heard. Dating couples lean closer to one another; voices rise (you can say something stupid and no one will know). A few restaurants take a more measured approach, introducing acoustic absorbent materials such as wall hangings, carpets, or acoustic ceiling tile, all of which make dinner conversations possible.

The shape of a room has a big impact on its acoustics, because sound waves bounce off walls just as light bounces off a mirror. Thus, when two walls are parallel to each other a sound wave can reflect from one wall to another several times before dissipating, creating unwanted echoes. A simple solution to this problem is to orient walls (and the ceiling) at slight angles to each other. A "whispering room" is an architectural folly that enables people at a distance from one another to communicate aurally via whispers that are focused by the surround-

---

[20] In a review of Frank Gehry's symphony hall, the New World Center in Miami, Alex Ross stated, "The acoustics certainly passed the foot test, which so many modern halls fail: during a fortissimo passage with rolling timpani, you could feel the floorboards trembling in sympathy." *The New Yorker*, February 14 and 21, 2011.

A and B are the two foci of the ellipse-shaped room. Standing at these two spots, a couple can hear each other whisper.

ing walls to each other. There are many historical examples of such spaces, including one at the Museum of Science and Industry in Chicago.

But there are also inadvertent examples of whispering rooms that have caused difficulties. The Statuary Hall at the U.S. Capitol was originally designed as the House of Representatives by the architects Latrobe, and later, Bulfinch in 1815. The plan is reminiscent of an ancient Greek amphitheater. This ancient plan worked well when a central speaker at the flat area spoke out to the audience arrayed outward in semi-circles. But the architects went wrong in two respects: First, the proceedings are not just the talk of one central actor, but also the conversations between the delegates themselves. Second, the plan was then covered with a hemispherical ceiling that bounced the speaker's voice back to him, not out to the audience. In short, the room proved acoustically unworkable and a new, alternate house was built in 1857. Today it is common for architects to consult with acoustical engineers who can recommend steps to alleviate potential acoustic problems and help create rooms with shapes and materials that will produce the desired acoustics.

AROMATIC DELIGHT: HOW DOES THE BUILDING SMELL?

You probably think we are going too far in suggesting that buildings can smell good. In fact, quite the opposite is all too often true, and the smell of modern materials (such as certain types of carpeting, paints, vinyl flooring, and foam insulation) can cause real discomfort to inhabitants and illness in some cases. This is because these materials can off-gas the solvents that were used in their manufacture for some time after installation, and these solvents can be quite toxic. A recent incident illustrates the problem: After the 2009 flooding in New Orleans the government provided trailers for temporary housing, but the people who tried to live in them soon became ill. It turned out that this was due to the off-gassing of the formaldehyde used in the construction process. In the end the trailers proved unusable.

In contrast to highly industrialized materials that make use of chemical processes in their manufacture, natural building materials most often have pleasant olfactory effects. Aside from those who have very sensitive reactions to ordinary elements, most people find the aroma of natural wood very pleasing, especially when newly milled and fresh. The same can be said of concrete, stone, rammed earth, linoleum, and fabrics of wool and cotton. Even a fireplace that retains a hint of smokiness can add to the pleasurable smell of a building. It has been said that ancient mosques were built with small amounts of deer musk embedded into their structures, the same musk that has been used for ages as the base of perfume. The thought was to make the mosque smell like heaven.

As materials age, their aromas change. European stone buildings have a distinct odor that speaks of old earth. One can hypothesize many alternate sources of this smell, but it is unmistakable when you are there. And it gives the same kind of pleasure that one gets from a wine that delivers the smell of its *terroir*, the soil and minerals out of which it grew.

Even the unpleasant smells that are generated in a building can be handled by good ventilation, to freshen the air and control humidity. The pleasurable smells of being in a building also come from the gardens and fresh air that surround it, which the building admits on its patios and through its windows and open doors. The building can integrate indoors and out, permitting use of both during good weather. One can smell rain, fall leaves burning, and fragrant flowering trees in spring. All of these will combine with the smells of the cooking and hobbies and collections of the inhabitants. But the building provides the underlying base smell upon which all else builds, like the key in which a piece of music is written.

INTELLECTUAL DELIGHT

This area of potential pleasure stems not from how we feel when we are in a building but rather from what the building makes us think about. Ideas and thoughts themselves can give pleasure, as when we recognize a new concept ("Aha, I get it!") or have an intuition reaffirmed and clarified. The most powerful architecture has the power to give us fresh and interesting new ideas. These insights can range from how the building is organized geometrically, functionally, or structurally, to gaining a more profound understanding of our culture and history. But intellectual reward is of quite a different order than visual delight. A new insight can be pleasurable, even delightful, as when a puzzle or a mathematical equation is solved. But it can also be sobering, stunning, even humbling, as when we really understand our mortality. A tragic play or a profound piece of music can be intellectually rewarding and deepening, even if we weep with empathy and understanding. So in this section on *venustas* we are broadening our sense of the word to include interest, understanding, and awe. Perhaps we should think of this as a profound sense of beauty.

To underscore this point, let's take two examples from the building type "memorial." The Vietnam Memorial by Maya Lin mentioned in Chapter 4 belongs to this type. Certainly, we don't ask that a memorial give us delight in the normal sense of the word, but we do expect that it will engage our mind and move us somehow, and memorials can move us in quite different ways. Arlington Memorial Cemetery in Washington, DC, provides a final resting place for those who have

served our country in the armed
forces, and the message of the arrangement of tombstones is one
of order, discipline, selfless sacri-
fice, and dignity. It is a memorial
to honorable deaths, given in the
defense of our country.

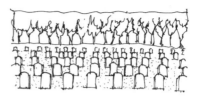

In contrast, the Holocaust
Memorial of 2005 in Berlin by
Peter Eisenman tells a very different story. First, the memorial elements—the individual
markers—are not stone tablets
marked with individuals' names,

At top, the Arlington Memorial Cemetery; below,
Holocaust Memorial, Berlin.

but coffin-like shapes of concrete bearing no names. It memorializes
the countless nameless victims whose remains will never be found.
And rather than a geometry of perfectly ordered, erect markers, Eisenman repeats identical forms but intentionally allows each to either
slightly heave up out of the unlevel ground or slightly sink down into it
in a random, unsettling manner.

The ground of this memorial is not the sweet green grass of Arlington that promises rebirth and renewal, but urban paving blocks
that speak of endless movement and lack of new roots. The design of
the Holocaust Memorial strikes us anew with the realization of the
countless lives lost, helplessly murdered rather than lost in battle,
whose proper interment will never be possible and whose spirits rest-
lessly heave and sink, seeking a just and honorable finale that can
never be realized.

So when we speak of intellectual delight we are talking about
the whole range of deep, profound ideas that we get from understanding something about the work—like the experience of listening to a
Bach fugue.

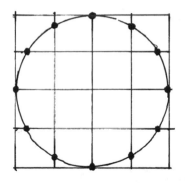

GEOMETRICAL TRUTHS

We explained earlier that the golden ratio produces a visually pleasing proportion. But in addition one can take pleasure in simply knowing that the proportion of a room plan or building facade is the mathematically interesting golden ratio. Geometry was established by the Greeks, and it played a central role in their conceptualization of city plans, building plans, and facades, even to the appearance of the heavens. Each integer and geometric solid was explored, related to each other, and linked to physical phenomena: the sizes and orbits of planets, musical scales, and, of course, proper dimensions for buildings.

Take the number 12, for instance, or *dodekad* in Greek (from "two ten"). It is the number that is divisible by 2, 3, 4, and 6 (making it very useful as the basis of the foot in the English measuring system, still used primarily in the United States). It also has some very surprising (and delightful) geometric properties. For example, although there are several easy ways to divide the circumference of a circle into 12 equal lengths, the method illustrated above is especially intriguing. A square is quartered in both dimensions, and a circle inscribed inside it. Where the quarter divisions fall upon the circle, the circle's circumference will be neatly divided into twelfths. Thus, the circle and the square can be united geometrically by these 12 equal divisions: This geometric fact could allow the columns of a building's rotunda to integrate with a rectangular grid in the rest of the building.

One of the purest architectural expressions of geometric truths is the proposed memorial for Isaac Newton designed by Etienne Nicholas Boullée in 1784. It takes the shape of a giant hollow sphere, nearly 500 feet in diameter. Newton's integrative laws of the motions of bodies—covering the falling apple as well as the heavenly bodies, his invention of the calculus, and his studies of light—all demanded a very special monument, one that embodied the precision, scope, and magnificence of his ideas.

The sphere would represent the heavens themselves, lit during the day by "starlight" that penetrated the sphere via small holes aimed up at the heavens, and lit at night by a huge sunlike light source at

THE POWER OF 12

A string with 12 equally spaced marks along its length can generate a right triangle, which is surprising unless one remembers that the Pythagorean triangle is made up of a 3-unit side, a 4-unit side, and the remaining 5-unit side. The area of this triangle is 6 (A = 3 × 4/2). What a wonderful, magical truth for the use of the architect in generating right angles directly on the site of a new building.

All of the integers from 1 to 13 were incorporated into Greek geometry and design and philosophy, but 12 is an especially interesting, useful, and profound number. Christian theology and Gothic design came together notably in the North Rose Window of Chartres Cathedral.

Perhaps the most recent architectural incorporation of 12's geometric properties is the cuboctahedron, a 12-packing of spheres surrounding a central embedded 13th sphere. It was dubbed the "dymaxion" by Buckminster Fuller, who could see the array as a packing of tetrahedrons, a perfect 3-dimensional truss system that could be repeatedly extended to roof over a space.

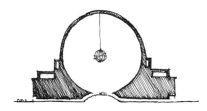

Boullée's Cenotaph for Isaac Newton.

the center. The scheme was fantastical (and full of unsolved problems) but the very idea of the building is breathtaking. It is almost better as a geometrical idea about a building than the actual one might have been. The building is composed of "perfect" geometries: a perfect sphere, sitting exactly halfway into two nested barrels. It shares the same basic geometry of the 1st-century Roman Pantheon.

There can be great aesthetic pleasure for those who can first glimpse, then later explore and understand, the underlying geometries that a building may be based on. Within the Euclidean framework, geometrical properties are somehow real, unchangeable, and true. As Keats wrote in the *Ode on a Grecian Urn*:

Beauty is truth, truth beauty,—That is all
Ye know on Earth, and all ye need to know.

The "Lightning Field" of 1977 by the artist Walter De Maria is a rectangular array of polished stainless-steel poles emerging vertically out of a natural desert field near Quemado, New Mexico. The poles are precisely 250 feet apart from each other, aligned on a grid 1 mile long by 1 kilometer wide. The poles are so far apart that wandering among them they feel randomly placed—that is until one looks down a single line of them, seeing that they are indeed organized in a grid. The experience of visiting the Lightning Field is profound, not just because one is "deposited" at the remote site overnight, not just because the poles' range is 1 kilometer by 1 mile (rather arbitrarily defined lengths), and not just that the array takes on amazingly different visual appearances at sunset and dawn. All of these aspects are wonderfully interesting, but the deepest concept inherent in the work is the virtual horizontal plane that is defined by the tops of the poles—each pole's length is

adjusted so that regardless of
the elevation of the hilly ground
below, the tips of the poles all
reach a single elevation. This
perfectly flat plane exists only
in one's mind, floating above
the varied floor of the desert
below. This geometric recogni-
tion brings deep pleasure. It has no purpose. It isn't a sermon, witticism,
or comment on modern Man's condition: It simply *is*, there for us to
contemplate and to hold in our attention as a meditation.

Diagram of The Lightning Field, New Mexico,
Walter DeMaria, 1977.

NATURALNESS

As the Greeks revered geometry, later European natural scientists
embraced nature's forms as the true source of beauty and truth. In the
early 1800s the Prussian Karl Wilhelm von Humboldt summarized
the significance of natural form:

> Natural objects themselves, even when they make no claim to beauty,
> excite the feelings, and occupy the imagination. Nature pleases, attracts,
> delights, merely because it is nature. We recognize in it an infinite power [21].

This suggests that the source of beauty (and delight) comes
directly from natural forms: If you want to make a beautiful building,
imitate the essential qualities found in the rock and wood from which
it is to be constructed. This imitation of qualities does not imply slav-
ish copies of the forms themselves—such as concrete railings cast into
the form of natural wooden logs. Such an approach soon wears thin.

John Ruskin's *The Seven Lamps of Architecture* of 1848 posited the
essential characteristics of beauty, which included the requirement

---

[21] From his *Letters to a Friend*, Leopzig, 1870.

that decorative carvings needed to follow nature. He asserted that
there were two aspects to nature: the forms and the process of their
creation by the artists. Ruskin argued that beautiful forms must have
their source in nature, and further, that the artist actually executing
the building and its carvings needed to be as responsive to the developing work as any growing organism is to the changing environment.

In 1917, D'Arcy Wentworth Thompson, an English explorer and
professor of natural history, published his book *On Growth and Form*,
in which he emphasized the growth process and the mechanical aspects of creating strong organisms. The study of nature suggests that
one might create beautiful buildings not by copying or imitating nature's forms, but rather by paying attention to the same geometrical,
structural, and growth processes that produce natural objects. After
all, isn't this how indigenous architecture is created? An individual
indigenous building is typically an example of a time-honored form. It
conforms to an established set of cultural and structural patterns, realized in response to a particular site and functional need. Finally, it is
built out of the natural local materials at hand, by the individual who

Thorsen House, Berkeley,
Greene & Greene, 1909.

will eventually inhabit the building. And aren't the results every bit as "natural" as organisms?

The American Arts and Crafts tradition produced buildings that did not try to look like nature but expressed the values of nature. Some examples include the work of Greene & Greene, Bernard Maybeck, and Julia Morgan, all working in California from the 1920s to the 1940s. The Greene brothers' 1909 Thorsen

The Chapel, Asilomar Conference Center, Julia Morgan, 1913.

House in Berkeley, California, uses the same overbaked slump bricks for the foundation of the building, the steps, the planters, and the walls. This gesture knits the building into the landscape, thereby expressing the idea that our buildings are not separate from nature.

Julia Morgan's several buildings at the Asilomar Conference Center in Carmel, California, are rooted to the ground with stone, planting, and wood. The chapel is an example of a building that seems to grow naturally out of its site.

The enthusiasm for natural form and process has taken many subsequent forms. The hippie culture of the 1960s and 1970s created hand-built structures out of more primitive materials, earth structures of adobe, rammed earth, and cob. Later, another quite different method of generating form arose in the schools of architecture developing structures that are capable of organic growth, change, and repair, made possible by the computer. This approach was dubbed "parametric architecture" or "generative architecture," and it suggests how a growth process utilizing underlying geometric and structural units can start to imitate natural organic forms.

The concept of generative design can be thought of in several ways. Throughout much of architectural history, curved forms have been

1. Opening network.

2. Create an entrance.

3. Pop out a bay window.

4. Have some fun with the roof and wall.

created out of many small identical blocks that are arranged with the loose spaces between them filled with mortar. But the computer has opened the possibility of designing with individually shaped, unique elements, each of which takes its specified place in the overall complex form.

In this process the architect tries to create natural form by beginning with a simple network of elements on the computer, then modifying the network to form the desired spaces. The computer continually recalculates the required size and shape of each element. Each piece is then automatically manufactured as directed by the computer. Each bears an identification number used to locate its proper place in the developing building. This process is powerful, giving the architect unprecedented design freedom.

In Chapter 4 we referred to several examples of this generative approach employed by the architects Gehry, Mayne, Hadid, and others. It isn't clear that this passion for parametricism, or generative architecture, always produces enduring and wonderful buildings.[22] What is obvious is that when architects are responsive to the site and the specific materials of construction, and they design buildings in an honest, straightforward manner, the buildings can start to be beautiful in a natural sense. They will feel that they are part of nature.

---

[22] Some critics agree: "Gestalt psychology's insights into perception (such as the preference for verticals and horizontals and perpendicular crossings that minimize the number of angles defined) explains why even if exciting, parametricism's forms are also fundamentally alienating." Peter Buchannan, *The Architectural Review*, October 2012, p. 97.

THE BEAUTY OF FUNCTIONAL AND STRUCTURAL CONCEPTS

In the last chapter we noted that *utilitas* alone can often give rise to great aesthetic pleasure. Throughout history this has continued to be an important theme in understanding beauty. For Quintilian, the 1st-century rhetorician, beauty was synonymous with utility:

> A horse whose flanks are compact is not only better to look upon, but swifter in speed. The athlete whose muscles have been formed by exercise is a joy to the eye, but he is also better fitted for the contests in which he must engage. In fact, true beauty and usefulness always go hand in hand.[23]

Sometimes buildings can teach us how they are conceived functionally or structurally. A striking example of this kind of intellectual communication is the Paris museum Centre Georges Pompidou designed in 1977 by Piano and Rogers (top drawing, p. 248). In this building the architects reveal to us the structure and the utilities (HVAC and pedestrian circulation) by pulling them out beyond the skin of the building, allowing the interior to remain open and uncluttered.

An earlier example of this same approach is the American architect Louis Kahn's formulation of served and service spaces, where he separated them for clarity. He did this first in his Richards Medical Research Building in Philadelphia, designed in 1957, where the stairs are exposed on the outside (bottom drawing, p. 248). In his later Salk Institute in La Jolla of 1959, also a research laboratory, he places these ample service spaces between the floors of the labs to facilitate future changes. The stairs remained vertical groupings at the exterior, and private offices were also stacked vertically facing the interior court.

The Centre Pompidou and these two buildings by Kahn emphasize the expression of structural and mechanical organization. They attempt

---

[23] From the *Institutio Oratoria of Quintilian*, Loeb Classical Library Edition, vol. 3, 1922, p. 217.

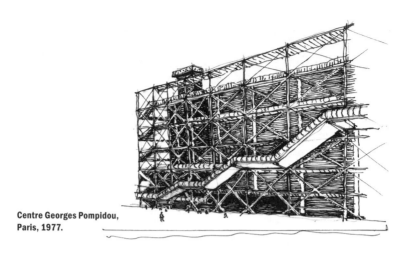

Centre Georges Pompidou, Paris, 1977.

to teach us about those aspects of a building that we don't normally think much about, and to explain this in an interesting and even profound manner. To the extent that we do learn something new, we get real intellectual delight from these buildings.

The social function of a building can also be expressed architecturally—and so vividly that we can take pleasure in "getting it." Architect Rudolph Schindler moved to southern California in 1920 to set up his own practice and build a house for himself. A visit to Yosemite inspired him to capture a bit of the primitive camping feel in his house: the primacy of fire, tent, and proximity to the ground. But he and his wife were also proto-hippies, bohemian, experimenters with new kinds of social organization. Along with another couple they designed an unusually functional two-family house, with individual studios for each

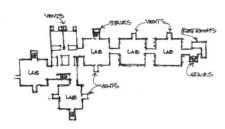

Richards Medical Research Building, Philadelphia, 1957.

of the four members of the group and one shared utility space at the center serving as kitchen and laundry for all. The plan eloquently shows all of this, with the studios for one couple forming an L-shaped wing facing a private court, with another L-shaped wing facing another private court. At the hinge of each L is a set of stairs leading up to an outdoor bedroom, or "sleeping basket."

Schindler's house is a sermon on sharing residential space, the central role of artistic creation in domestic life, and the need to stay in touch

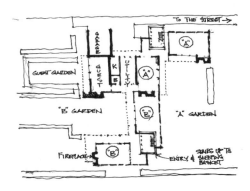

Schindler's Kings Road House, Los Angeles, 1922.

with the earth and weather. These are the intentions expressed by the design. Whether it in fact functions as well as intended is another matter. In this case the original inhabitants didn't stay together in the house for long. The architectural significance of the building, and the source of our intellectual pleasure, lies in the clarity of its intended function rather than how well it actually functions.

EMOTIONAL DELIGHT: HOW DOES THE BUILDING MAKE YOU FEEL?

No matter what an architect is attempting to "say" with the design of a building, no matter what aspects of aesthetic delight have been included in the building—whether they be visual, aural, tactile, thermal, or intellectual—the actual experience of the building will evoke emotions in the observer that the architect has no control over. Even if the observer of the building understands perfectly well the aesthetic elements that have been built into the structure, the resulting emotional response belongs to the observer alone. You can visit a building that has absolutely no charm at all—with no visual merit, no interesting aspects—and still have a positive emotional response to it because of any number of personal factors. The charmless building might remind you of your childhood home, or of a place where you remember having a pleasant experience. Equally, a building full of the kinds of potential pleasure outlined above might be experienced with very negative emotions because of difficult or painful memories it may evoke. Each visitor to a building brings along a complex of associations that relate to past conditioning and experience.

Our emotional responses to a building stem from what we are thinking about in terms of the building, or our particular relationship to it given our different social role or life situation. The architecture of Rome felt different to a wealthy and influential citizen than it did to a servant or slave. The architecture of Berlin's Tempelhof airport stirs different emotions in the technical aircraft enthusiast than it does in the victim of Germany's World War II activities, or in the recipients of food and supplies flown there during the Berlin airlift (and these conflicting emotions can even occur in the same individual).

Because only a small percentage of the buildings in the United States have been designed by architects,[24] and even many of those are not necessarily outstanding examples of architecture, by far the majority of our experience is with "background" buildings, as critic Paul Goldberger coined them. Yet these are the buildings that we have grown up with, become used to, and, as a result, are emotionally comfortable with. We demand that our buildings be structurally sound, that they work well for our purposes, and we ask that they be reasonably pleasant to look at. By and large we want to be comfortable with the aesthetics of our buildings. But that doesn't necessarily involve wanting to be aesthetically challenged by them, or confronted with new and unfamiliar ideas.

This is a sad fact that must be accepted by architects, who have developed refined and educated senses of the potential artistic plea-

---

[24] The percentage has ranged from 2 percent to around 25 percent, but it all depends on how you figure. What about the buildings that copy an architect's design? Or an architect's design that is repeated hundreds of times in a subdivision?

sures that buildings can offer, but who often serve clients who are less open to experimentation with new and vivid experiences. These less adventurous clients above all seek comfort: comfort with how their project fits into the neighborhood and city, comfort with the budget, and comfort with the tastefulness of the design. The architect may know how to provide all this architectural comfort food, but may feel frustrated by the inability to push the envelope, to do a more exciting, interesting, provocative design, one that might explore and express new ideas. Thus the emotional delight of the client can often be at odds with the creative delight sought by their architect. The obvious solution is a more collaborative design process, a joint creation by client and architect.

Feeling comfortable with the appearance of a building is an emotion governed partly by the physical pleasures offered by the building, by what the inhabitant thinks about the building's firmness, commodity, and delight, by what the building reminds one of, or by what the building signifies (such as the status and social position of the inhabitants), and even by how one is feeling at the moment. Pleasure is often simply a result of good digestion.

But fortunately for architects, some clients seek, beyond mere comfort, a more stimulating and awakening experience from their buildings. This is the architect's dream: a client who asks to be surprised, aroused, invigorated, even challenged by the building's design. In such collaborations the architect can attempt a deeper, perhaps more universal and profound design process. Even when a client doesn't want to be transported by their building, the architect may aim higher, hoping that the greater public will be excited by the structure. Louis Kahn once wrote to a client that he hoped she would be happy with the design for her house, but later confided to his private journal that he didn't really have a client until he had produced something of general significance for mankind, his ultimate client.

Denver Art Museum, Daniel Libeskind, 2006.

The feeling of civic pride might encourage a city government to hire a "starchitect" to design their city buildings, hoping that a courageous, bold, exciting design will put their town more firmly on the map. The 2006 addition to Denver's Art Museum designed by Daniel Libeskind joins neighboring buildings—the earlier gray, windowless art museum by Gio Ponti to the left and the Postmodern building behind by Michael Graves—upstaging them both with a wild collision of sharp metallic forms.

Kansas City chose New York-based architect Steven Holl for a similarly dramatic addition to their Nelson-Atkins museum, a half-sunken complex sheathed in translucent glass that glows at night. In these examples, communities are seeking a new emotional sense of importance, direction, and vision. They want to be proud of their city via a landmark building that will bring wide attention.

But individuals can also experience the emotion of pride in their buildings, not only their civic buildings, but their own neighborhoods and homes. This can be especially true for those individuals who have either designed or built their own home, or who have taken a major role in its design along with their architect. They will take pride in the fact that the building was designed around their needs and wishes—a custom design just for them.

Buildings can also give rise to negative feelings and emotions. They may exceed our capacity to understand them, or even to understand how to use them, creating unpleasant nervous and fearful emotions, like when we get lost in a strange neighborhood and can't get oriented. They can even overexcite us, leading us to dizzyingly high edges of balconies or carrying us up in glass elevators that undermine our feeling of safety and literally make us fearful. Or they might be so unimaginative that we find ourselves depressed looking at their blank facades.

Yet we need to remember that our emotion associated with a building is partly a result of thinking and attitude, not a direct result of the place itself. The ride up 30 stories in a glass elevator will thrill one passenger, who thinks that he is perfectly safe, allowing an enjoyable openness to the flying, free sensation, whereas his fellow passenger, unconvinced of his safety, will get as far away from the glass as possible and remain simply terrified during the trip. Thus the architect, especially when designing a public building, is faced with a dilemma: The attempt to create delight through powerful stimulation of all the senses may generate widely differing emotions. At the appropriate level of a building's novelty, stimulation, and uniqueness, most of us will be able to feel energized, awakened, and hopefully delighted. At the extremes, some will be delighted, others horrified.

THE UNITY OF *FIRMITAS, UTILITAS,* AND *VENUSTAS*

In this final chapter we have touched upon the many architectural qualities that contribute to *venustas*, starting with the visual elements of order and variety, proportion, scale, clarity, and harmony. But we have also extended and broadened the concept of *venustas* to include the haptic, acoustic, and aromatic avenues to architectural delight. Furthermore, we have stressed that architecture can offer intellectual pleasure through the expression of geometric truths as well as significant structural and functional ideas. Finally, we have seen that architecture can generate emotional pleasure via references to our memory and history.

Thus our response to *venustas* can include visual fascination, but also sensual delight as well as intellectual and emotional pleasure. Architecture can generate intense interest and excitement, awe and reverence, sadness, and deep peace.

While the notion of *venustas* has evolved throughout history, we are also keen to understand and appreciate the role of *venustas* in Vitruvius's triad today. In the Introduction we offered the Borromeo knot as a symbol of the triadic relationship between *firmitas, utilitas,* and *venustas,* stating our belief that the absence of any one results in the dissolution of the architectural knot. A building that lacks *firmitas* cannot long survive, one that lacks *utilitas* will be abandoned, while one that lacks *venustas* may continue to serve but will not be treasured without the sustaining spirit that elevates it to the realm of architecture.

In conclusion, we offer the additional notion that the trio must be in balance, working together to create a unified and coherent result. But we recognize that in practice they are not typically in perfect balance; usually there is more emphasis on one or another. When Frank Lloyd Wright designed furniture for his houses he leaned heavily in the direction of *venustas* (at the expense of *utilitas*), harmonizing the design of the chairs with that of the building more than with the need of the body for a comfortable seat. And among today's most renowned architects the artistic impulse often takes front row and center. Architects within this group (Gehry, Hadid, Eisenman, Libeskind, Koolhaas, Mayne, et al.) not only consider themselves talented architects but also Artists with a capital "A." Their buildings are unmistakably "theirs," stamped with their unique personality and style, and the buildings tend to stand out on their own as remarkable statements, sometimes independent of the country, town, or neighborhood in which they are located, and seemingly independent of their intended function. To speak plainly, these esteemed architects often create forms that promise *venustas* as the primary goal, letting structure (and sometimes utility) serve that end.

Another attitude that may favor one aspect over another stems from the philosophy of the "naturalists" set forth by Humboldt—and his notion that, without trying to be beautiful, the processes of organic growth inevitably lead to beautiful forms. We have similarly recognized in this chapter that a focus on *firmitas* and *utilitas* alone can often produce *venustas*. In fact, the designers of industrial and commercial buildings typically focus on ensuring that the structure is sound and economical and that the functional needs are met. They often assume that the aesthetic issue is either irrelevant or that it will automatically take care of itself. And sometimes it will, as evidenced by such structures as the Eiffel Tower, the Crystal Palace, or the many glass-roofed train stations, grain silos, and barns of the 19th and 20th centuries. Actually, this is not a bad strategy for the early stages of architectural design: Don't worry for the time being about how the building is going to look, about whether it will be attractive, or whether it will get published in the architectural journals; get the functional and structural basics right, and then take a look at the result in terms of aesthetics. It might be just fine.

But there is a better way to create architecture, namely bringing in each of the three aspects to work cooperatively with each other from the start, letting each influence the others, preventing any one of them from dominating. We believe that the most beautiful and satisfying architecture emerges from this integration of Vitruvius's triad, where each aspect reinforces and contributes to the whole. This is as true of indigenous architecture as it is of the Gothic cathedrals or the best contemporary work. This unity of intention, and purity of purpose, where each aspect is working together, is a prerequisite for genuine architecture, for places that satisfy our deepest needs, for places that are beautiful in the most profound and significant sense. □

CODA

WE BEGAN THIS INVITATION TO ARCHITECTURE by recommending travel and exploration of new buildings to awaken and refresh our readiness and appetite for architecture. And we've offered updated versions of Vitruvius's *firmitas, utilitas,* and *venustas,* a toolkit of criteria that we all can use to better observe, experience, and understand architecture. We've also shown how these three dimensions are interdependent with one another in architecture.

On a recent trip to the Northwest we decided to take our own advice and explore the effectiveness of this approach. We decided to stop along the way in Seattle for a day and visit two buildings that we had read about that promised to be interesting. And we would view them through the trio of Vitruvian lenses. We would ask the following questions: Do the aesthetics of the building (its visual organization, proportion, color, feel, and overall mood or idea) harmonize and underscore its function? Does the building's structure facilitate and support the intended functions of its users (or frustrate and hinder them)? Are the structural members visually interesting, perhaps even explanatory of their role in creating *firmitas,* thereby contributing to our aesthetic appreciation of the building?

Seattle is an exciting, forward-looking city, full of tourists eager to ascend the Space Needle, visit Pike Place Market, and enjoy the Experience

Music Project. The 2004 Seattle Library by Dutch architect Rem Koolhaas has joined the other must-see attractions of the city by virtue of its very dramatic design. It was widely publicized when completed, and our interest was especially piqued by a more recent post-occupancy review.[1] A quite different building, the 2013 Bullitt Office Center by the Seattle firm of Miller/ Hull, has also received good press,[2] primarily because it is touted as the "greenest," most sustainable building in America.

As you drive downtown, the library suddenly looms into view, looking like a cross between an alien space station that has crumpled a bit upon landing and a giant steel and glass irregularly faceted transparent geode. In terms of *venustas*, its exterior doesn't relate to or harmonize with its surroundings but rather sets off a shock wave of surprise—we've simply never seen a building cover a whole city block with a shape like this! It is mysterious, awe-inspiring. At a height of 11 stories, the enormous external greenhouse covers and contains over half a million square feet of floor space inside. From the outside the building doesn't exude *firmitas*—firm, strong stability—so much as a momentary pause before taking off again. Some wall sections of glass exhibit a kind of *utilitas* as they loom over the southern entrance, functionally acting as a kind of protective roof. But the uniform steel and glass exterior makes no other gestures toward the func-

tion of entering a major building, or even helping to find those entries, which are so small and understated as to be overlooked, even missed.

A different world opens up inside. There, one encounters a riot of visual (and physical) stimulation:

[1] "Overexposed," by Witold Rybczynski, in *Architect*, April 2013.

[2] "Going Beyond Green," by Bryn Nelson, *New York Times*, April 3, 2013, p. B1. "A Deeper Shade of Green," by Joann Gonchar, *Architectural Record*, June 2013, pp. 217–224.

vast volumes penetrated by diagonal steel columns shooting through the spaces, upper floors cantilevering out from a central concrete core, an 11-story-high atrium shaft of empty space, a complex network of stairs and escalators in Jello®-yellow, and a sinuously winding fourth floor totally bathed in blood red (including the floor, walls, ceiling, and fixtures), like the inside of a human heart. This building is full-on exciting, stunning, and even a little frightening.

To be a little more analytical, we need not fret about the actual *firmitas* of the building. Its structure is designed by highly skilled engineers, and it meets strict building codes. The problem, if it is a problem, is that the structure is so complicated that only structural engineers can fully understand and appreciate how it works. The rest of us are so dazzled by the variety of structural elements (vertical columns, slanted columns, cantilevered floors, trusses, the diamond ribbed structure of the glass skin, and so on) that we simply marvel at the complexity, say "Wow!," and leave it at that. We suspect that Koolhaas wants us to be baffled and awed by the structure.

Neither is the *utilitas*, or functionality, of the building particularly simple. The building is being asked to do many things. For starters, the city selected Koolhaas because it wanted to take pride in another tourist attraction, while the leaders of the library wanted to reinvigorate the whole notion of what a library could be. Both parties wanted a cutting-edge facility

that was shaped around the digital world of information as much as around books. So, in a sense, as one looks at the usefulness of the building it is necessary to reset one's expectations. With its acres of computer stations, WIFI capability, a staff prepared to answer any questions, coffee and snack shop, gift store, and a multitude of open sitting areas for relaxation, this is a new kind of facility that functions as much as a social center, tourist attraction, homeless shelter, and WIFI hotspot as it does as a conventional library of books.

While the building works as a futuristic library, it suffers from at least one important dysfunction: It isn't immediately clear how to access and get around the place. For us personally it was impossible to get a coherent mental image of the building's spatial and circulation organization—and we're architects! The staff tell the same story: They spend too much time helping visitors find their way around. Again, it seems that the architect relished the complexity of organization, thinking perhaps that disorientation adds to a bubbly kind of thrill.

So if we are amazed by the structural complexity but don't understand it, and if we can have all sorts of useful and fun activities but sometimes get lost finding them, where does this leave *venustas*, the aesthetic element? Clearly the aesthetics don't emerge from the clarity of structure and function, like a Gothic cathedral; nor can the library's aesthetics be described as economical, ordered, well proportioned, or coherent. Instead, the delight grows out of the shear amazement that the variety and complexity command. Importantly, the building is consistently unique and provocative in all its Vitruvian aspects, challenging, and awe-inspiring in the scale of its "chutzpa." If we could forget that it is a strong and safe structure, and that it is functional in many unconventional ways (and dysfunctional in some of the ordinary ones), we could view it as a very creative work of Art by an artist who had the presence of mind to follow a strong personal vision. But to express that vision in the form of a firm and useful building is to do architecture, not Art.

Not surprisingly, the building has been controversial. Herbert Muschamp, the *New York Times* architecture critic at the time of its opening, gushed, "In more than 30 years of writing about architecture, this is the most exciting new building it has been my honor to review," while Heidi Burkhardt, a Seattle local, wrote to the library, "Who are the people in Seattle who have collectively taken some ugly pills?"[3] Controversy is healthy

---

[3] Both quotes from *Seattle Post-Intelligencer*, May 20, 2004.

for architecture, keeping people interested and involved. If attendance and use matters, the building is a great success. On balance, we judge it to be more stimulating, exciting, humorous, and fun than you could ever imagine a library to be. It is delightfully outrageous, and we are grateful that we had the opportunity to visit, enjoy, and criticize it.

And now to the Bullitt Center. There are so many ways that architecture can please (and occasionally dismay) us. The thrill of the Library's "bad boy" edgy surprises is so different from the calm and sober effect of the Bullitt Center, which, at a mere tenth the size of the Library, offers a rarer and perhaps more meaningful pleasure. One appreciates that the building has something important to teach us, something that is "right" in a new way, a quality that we haven't seen before, or that our culture has long ago forgotten.

At first glance, the exterior of the building looks normal enough, perhaps even ordinary: a metal and glass glazing system, a restrained six-story prism that only varies its shape to express a major stairway and an exterior balcony. Unlike the library, the exterior is not trying to make an exciting aesthetic statement. Rather its *venustas* comes from restraint, balance, and a simple rhythmic order. The exterior doesn't reveal much about the *firmitas* of the building, as the glazing system covers all the real structure inside. Nor does it tell us about *utilitas*, about the building's role. But wait, what is

that strange flat "hat" at the roof that extends in places 20 feet out beyond the building? To make a long and wonderful story short, Bullitt is touted as the world's "greenest" building, and this "mortar board" cap supports all the PVC panels required to supply the building's electrical needs. So in this sense our first glimpse of the roof, and our further observation of the sunshades outside each window that automatically withdraw to allow the sun's warmth to heat the interior when required, start to illustrate and explain the building's sustainable mission, an important key to Bullitt's overall *utilitas*.[4]

The *firmitas* of the building starts to be apparent as you move inside, with the first two stories of exposed poured concrete and the upper stories of exposed engineered wood and diagonal steel ties. All the upper floors align vertically and have the same plan, permitting a very simple straightforward post and beam layout that we can immediately grasp and understand. This unusual choice of materials for the structure of an office building addresses the overall goal of sustainability. The engineered wood posts and beams utilize wood waste that has been physically and chemically bound together to form large, strong pieces—and Washington has lots of local waste wood at hand. Similarly, the region has always had a strong steel industry, enabling local manufacture of that component. Thus, the structure and the overall mission cooperate—*firmitas* and *utilitas* work together.

In terms of *utilitas*, the Bullitt's use is as an office building, but more important, its function is to be a daring demonstration of how to make a commercially viable yet sustainable off-the-grid building. All water comes from the sky and all sewage is composted in the basement. Ground-source heating and cooling, along with natural daylighting, flesh out the yearly energy needs. And as an experiment, its effectiveness will be thoroughly recorded and evaluated over time. Assuming that it performs as hoped (saving 80 percent of the energy normally used in a comparable building), it is intended to inform and influence future construction in our country. So another of its uses is to teach us all how to put together a truly green project: The exhibit lobby space on the first floor displays all the building's vitals, including incoming and outgoing electrical energy, water supply, temperature, and humidity. Another display illustrates how 2,100 building products were analyzed to eliminate 14 common but toxic components. This restriction required reformulation by manufacturers and suppli-

---

[4] The Bullitt Center is the first substantially sized existing American building that complies with the rigorous Living Building Challenge, a set of criteria that defines an unprecedented high level of sustainability.

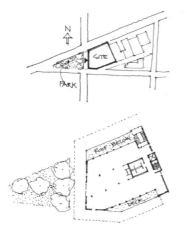

ers who wanted to join the green revolution train. And the building is designed for a 250-year lifespan, with accessible machinery and siding that can be repaired over time if necessary. There's a lot more to the sustainability aspect of Bullitt's *utilitas*, like the unprecedented reliance upon the composting toilets, but you get the picture.

Besides the building's use as a "green" icon, *utilitas* is apparent in the design and layout of the floor plans and other amenities. The major stairway, for example, is designed to be so irresistible (given the spectacular views of the surrounding mountains and water) compared to the plain, small elevator (only accessible with a key card), that everyone will be inspired to walk up, strengthening hearts and clearing arteries while saving energy. Each floor is laid out with the restrooms, kitchens, stairs, and elevator clustered on the northeast, freeing up the work spaces to be lit by natural light from the other three sides of 14-foot-high window walls. Each of the identical upper four floors has access to openable triple-glazed windows and a giant sliding glass door fully opening to the adjacent park and the larger city beyond. Internal temperature is allowed to vary a bit with the weather, and workers are allowed to adjust their immediate microclimate with the openable windows. A look at the typical floor plan illustrates how the structure helps to define the use of space: The necessary internal posts are organized along the center of the floor along with a kitchenette, encouraging this central area to work as meeting space and more private offices, leaving the bulk of the area for general workspace, close to the light from the windows. All of these design features create calm, quiet, well-lit spaces, an effective and supportive workplace. Again, *firmitas* working with *utilitas*.

But an even happier story is the building's *venustas*. The interior has an unusual kind of beauty—simple, honest, and clear. The exposed concrete work of the structure and floor topping is careful, down to earth, but not fussy. The same feeling is generated by the naturally warm golden brown wooden structural posts, beams, and floor/ceiling framing. The exposed black steel connectors and open tension rods proudly display their nuts and bolts, keeping no secrets. Even the mechanical rooms with their exquisitely clean and organized piping, tanks, and pumps bring joy to anyone who appreciates beautiful machinery.

This is an architecture of high dignity and clear intent. The extra-high ceilings (to allow deeper penetration of light), together with the unadorned natural materials and the soft "oyster light" of the Pacific Northwest filling the space, combine to create a deep calm, a noble sense of purposefulness and order. The Bullitt Center demonstrates that a purity of intent, guided by a vision of how the city and its structures might transform themselves in the future, can lead to a form of reverence, a faith in a better future.

We spent only a couple of hours in each of these two buildings on our exploratory visits, but the reward was great—we were stirred by both. They enlarged our appreciation for the architectural skills that went into each building. And we were reminded how rewarding it can be to encounter the buildings around us anew, with a fresh open eye. The Seattle Library and the Bullitt Center couldn't contrast more sharply, but by focusing on *firmitas*, *utilitas*, and *venustas* we were better able to understand how each aspect was being dealt with and integrated into the architecture.

Our Invitation to Architecture remains always open. For our part, we will continue to venture into new places that can enrich our growing store of environmental experience and will try to tease out how these places work using our Vitruvian tools of analysis. We hope you will join us in exploring the built world around us.

INDEX